INTRODUCING SHAKESPEARE TO YOUNG PEOPLE

by Priscilla Morris

GW00381632

OBERON BOOKS
LONDON

First published in 1996 by Oberon Books Ltd in association with the London Academy of Music and Dramatic Art.

Copyright London Academy of Music and Dramatic Art © 1996

ISBN 1 870259 72 6

Cover design: Andrzej Klimowski

Cover typography: Richard Doust

PRISCILLA MORRIS

PRISCILLA MORRIS, LGSM, LLCM, LLAM (Hons), ALAM, was a member of the National Youth Theatre, appearing in *Zigger Zagger* and *Fuzz*. She subsequently trained at the Guildhall School of Music and Drama. In 1972 she founded her own drama school in the Midlands where she continues to teach children and adults at all levels. Since joining LAMDA's Board of Examiners in 1986, she has examined throughout Great Britain and Ireland as well as internationally. She is also an adjudicator in Speech and Drama for the British Federation of Festivals, for whom she has worked all over Britain and abroad. Priscilla runs courses in Business Communication as well as practical workshops in all areas of performance. She is particularly in demand for her Practical Shakespeare workshops which have been given in many locations, including Singapore and Bermuda. When time permits, she enjoys acting and directing, as well as music, collecting dolls and tapestry.

PRISCILLA MORRIS

CONTENTS

PROLOGUE

"Oh, not Shakespeare, Miss – it's boring."

"What's the point in doing that, it's so old fashioned?"

"I don't understand it. What does it mean?"

How many times, I wonder, have teachers been faced with those familiar cries and wondered how to get over this seemingly insurmountable barrier? Many young people consider Shakespeare to have no relevance to modern life or learning – and yet he is unquestionably our greatest playwright. How disheartening to think of the large number of school-leavers who have had no contact with this rich dramatic source, a number which is, sadly, increasing annually.

As LAMDA teachers and students we have an opportunity to redress the balance. Shakespeare's words were written to be "performed" not read, often without expression, by a bored class of teenagers. They can be brought to life in a myriad of different ways.

My brief, in writing this book, is to give you ideas on how to enthuse your students and hopefully give them an appreciation of how enjoyable studying Shakespeare can be.

All you need is an open mind, a little imagination and a lot of energy!

BEGINNINGS

Let us from point to point this story know,
To make the even truth in pleasure flow.

All's Well That Ends Well, Act V, Sc: iii

I have often been asked, "At what age can students cope with Shakespeare?" My answer is from quite an early age, providing you present it to them in the right way.

LAMDA's introduction of Shakespeare in the Verse and Prose syllabus at grade 7 suggests that the original text is left until the age of twelve or thirteen. However, we mustn't forget what marvellous stories Shakespeare told in his plays. These can be introduced at a much younger age. Let's look at what can be achieved with juniors.

A MIDSUMMER NIGHT'S DREAM

A number of stories lend themselves very well to class work with middle juniors. The play which obviously springs to mind is *A Midsummer Night's Dream.* Here we have all the elements which appeal to young imaginations – fairies, magic and comedy. How can we stimulate their interest without resorting to a full-length reading of the story – although this can of course be attempted?

Isolate the sub-plot of the argument between Titania and Oberon. Here you have a range of possibilities: to explore the characters of the Fairy King, Queen and Puck – the lower order fairies – the comic figure of Bottom – arguments – the magic of a supernatural spell – not to mention a fairy song and possibilities for dance and movement.

So, armed with a basic knowledge of this sub-plot, the class can follow a number of avenues:

Using Movement

Explore how fairies might move. How can you make them non-human? You might like to use music here.

There are of course obvious choices, such as the incidental music to *A Midsummer Night's Dream* by Mendelssohn, but almost any music will do. The suggestion that the fairies are extremely naughty and mischievous can result in some hilarious expressions and movements if a free rein is given. Might I suggest that, in order to avoid total chaos, each fairy is given an individual entrance and his or her own short sequence of music to express him or herself. You can then allow the whole class to come together at the end.

Perhaps you might use masks here to stimulate further imaginative response. I have let the fairies "transform" into animals to torment Bottom before Titania wakes. A range of plastic or cardboard masks (the latter could, of course, be made by the children) might lead to an exploration of animal movement and, by incorporating music, to simple dance sequences. Link this to the arrival of Bottom, complete with ass's head, and you have linked two elements of the story.

Using Song

Shakespeare's plays contain a great deal of music. This can be a boon to teachers working with large classes. In the sequence we are working on, we have Titania's lullaby, "You Spotted Snakes". This delightful song has words which appeal very much to the young student – with its references to "creepy crawlies" of every description, from "beetles black" to "long-legged spinners". There are a number of published tunes to these words or you may wish to compose your own. Whatever decision you make, you can be sure the children will enjoy learning to sing it. Don't forget to remind them that fairies sing in a special way – not like humans! Once the song is learned, incorporate movement into the sequence and let the fairies cover Titania with leaves and sing her to sleep in her bower.

You should use the words of "You Spotted Snakes" as written in the play – these are not difficult to understand.

The rest of the scene, beginning with the argument between Titania and Oberon and ending with Bottom waking up in confusion and Oberon releasing Titania from the charm, can be improvised in modern English.

Using Art and Design

A great deal of fun can be had by allowing the class to design their own fairy costumes. These can be done in any form – collage is particularly good as they can explore texture as well as colour and form. It is important that the children bear in mind that they would need to be able to move in them – this will avoid the over-use of metal and similar substances. I once saw a design for Titania which bore more resemblance to a transformer than a fairy! These designs need never be converted to real costumes, of course. We are simply instilling in young minds the beginnings of an understanding of how costumes are used on stage, how they can suggest character and affect movement.

Those of you who work in private practice might think that I have ignored your needs so far – but look again at the ideas I have put forward and see how they can be adapted for small groups or solo tuition. You can still look at fairy movement, costume design and learn the song. Of course you cannot act out the whole sub-plot, but you can use the story as a stimulus for improvisation based on the number of students taking part. You can even write a solo scene or short duologue using the theme of an argument resolved by supernatural means.

Using Make-up

Until recently, using theatrical make-up involved using greasepaint, which made it difficult for young children to manage. Now there are a number of water-based products available which can be applied using brushes and washed off with soap, which makes them much easier to use in class.

I have found Grimas products very good. They produce palettes which give a good range of colours and enable children to experiment on each other and themselves while learning the basics of theatrical make-up. Grimas also produce booklets which give instructions on how to achieve different looks: including animals, fantasy, period and ageing. Some of these can be fitted very easily into your play study.

If you wanted to study *A Midsummer Night's Dream* further, you could work on the play within a play – *Pyramus and Thisbe*. This provides opportunities to create the comic characters of the mechanicals and could again lead to costume design for Wall, Moonshine etc. The story is readily converted into modern English but you might be surprised at the ease with which top juniors will take to the original rhyming couplets: they are fun to say and give lots of opportunity for over-acting!

Other plays and sub-plots which lend themselves to junior work include *The Comedy of Errors* with its double case of mistaken identity: explore the problems this creates when neither twin knows that the other exists! *Macbeth* has three witches cooking up a spell. This is quite an obvious choice and you might like to incorporate it into a themed concert on the supernatural, complete with appropriate costumes and props!

FILMS AND BOOKS

An excellent way to introduce the stories to top juniors is to use the *Animated Tales* series of videos. These highly imaginative films condense the text to about twenty-five minutes, which means that only the most accessible elements of the story are used and the students are introduced to the story and the language in a visually stimulating way. At the time of writing, there are twelve plays available in the series. I would particularly recommend *The Tempest* (for its supernatural quality), *Macbeth* (very atmospheric, although quite frightening at times) and *Romeo and Juliet* (a beautiful version of this classic love story).

There are several modern versions of Shakespeare stories which I have detailed at the end of this chapter. Teachers of juniors might like to include some of these in class reading sessions. Remember that if you can interest children at this age it will be relatively easy to move on to the actual text in performance when they begin high school.

For those sceptics among you who still wonder whether young children can fully appreciate Shakespeare let me relate an experience I had with an eight year old student a few years ago.

As part of my annual week's Summer School, I always take a party of students to the Royal Shakespeare Theatre at Stratford. This particular year we were going to see a matinée performance of *The Tempest*, with a lecture on the play with slides beforehand at the Education Centre. Most of the students who had enrolled for the day were aged twelve to eighteen, but the mother of one eight year-old girl asked if she could join us – she was very keen to see her first Shakespeare play. I agreed, with the proviso that she would need to know a little about the story and characters to help her understand the action. On the morning of our trip we began by watching the *Animated Tales* version of the story, then travelled to Stratford and gathered at the Education Centre for our lecture. The lecturer began by asking some simple questions about the play and went on to talk in more detail about the plot and how directors at the RSC have treated it. When questions were asked, the eight year old's hand was always up first with detailed information about characters and plot, leaving her fellow students – and even the lecturer – open-mouthed. It transpired that her mother had taken the time to hire an *Animated Tales*, watched it herself with her daughter a couple of times and read the story to fill in any gaps. As a result, the young lady went on to watch the play itself with rapt attention and gained a great deal from the whole experience. She has since watched several more Shakespeare plays and is eager for the day when she is old

put her knowledge to use in examination work.
...rhaps we, as teachers, should adopt the motto "You're
never too young."

BOOK LIST

The publications I list at the end of each chapter are by no
means exhaustive. They are simply books which I have found
useful in teaching. The following list would be particularly
helpful when teaching juniors:

William Shakespeare, Geoffrey Earle, (Ladybird Books)

Tales from Shakespeare, Charles and Mary Lamb, (Everyman)

Stories from Shakespeare, Marchette Chute, (John Murray)

Shakespeare Stories (2 volumes), Leon Garfield, (Victor
    Gollancz Ltd)

Songs from Shakespeare, (Walker Books)

The Animated Tales (2 illustrated volumes), Leon Garfield,
    (Heinemann)

TIME AND THE MAN

Come what come may,
Time and the hour runs through the roughest day.

Macbeth Act I, Scene iii

EXAMINER: Could you tell me when Shakespeare
was writing?

CANDIDATE: Er – well it was – er – in the
nineteenth century wasn't it?

You might find it hard to believe that this was an actual answer
in examination conditions but, amazingly, I have been offered
almost every alternative – from "the middle ages" to "early
twentieth century." Surely this is essential information for any
student of Shakespeare.

I feel strongly that you cannot fully understand the plays
without having some knowledge of the playwright and the
times in which he lived. There are often direct references in
the text to contemporary events and people, and
Shakespeare's drawing of a character may be coloured by
political considerations or a wish to please his audience with
a topical reference. Before embarking on individual plays it
is helpful, if time allows, for the private student or class to
undertake a project on Shakespeare's life.

LIFE HISTORY

You can start with the vast selection of biographical books
available at most libraries. Perhaps a list of dates showing the
major events of his life and times would come in useful:

1558	Accession of Elizabeth I
1564	23rd April – William Shakespeare born
1582	Shakespeare married Anne Hathaway
1583	Daughter Susanna born
1585	Twins Hamnet and Judith born

1585-91	The 'lost' years
1592	Shakespeare listed as an actor with the Lord Chamberlain's Company
1592	Shakespeare's first play *Henry VI Part I* performed
1592-94	Theatres closed due to Bubonic Plague
1596	Hamnet died aged 11
1597	Shakespeare's new wealth allowed him to buy New Place in Stratford
1599	The opening of the Globe Theatre
1603	Elizabeth I died. James I succeeded
1603	Lord Chamberlain's men became the King's Men
1605	The Gunpowder Plot
1607	Susanna married Dr John Hall
1609	The King's Men performed at the indoor Blackfriars Theatre for the winter season
1610	Shakespeare probably returned to live in Stratford
1612/13	The Globe Theatre burned down
1616	23rd April – Shakespeare died

When you tie up these dates with the plays written at certain times in his life, you begin to find some interesting links:

- Shakespeare was probably well-acquainted with his contemporary, Christopher Marlowe. He used elements of the plot of Marlowe's *The Jew of Malta* in *The Merchant of Venice* and he would certainly have been shocked by Marlowe's violent early death in 1593 in a tavern brawl. Shakespeare referred to Marlowe in *As You Like It* as "the dead Shepherd"

- The patriotic fervour seen in *Henry V* was certainly an act of diplomacy by Shakespeare during the reign of a Tudor Queen. The Chorus speaks about the campaigns of the Earl of Essex in Ireland at the time. The Elizabethan audiences would have fully understood these contemporary references

- Richard III is portrayed as an evil hunchback – not the upright, thoughtful monarch we think him now. Shakespeare based his play on Sir Thomas More's history of the last Plantagenet king, which, for the first time, depicted Richard as a monster. This was an expedient characterisation for writers living under Tudor rule – monarchs who were direct descendants of Richard's conqueror!

- The wreck of the ship, "Sea Adventure", off Bermuda in 1609 provided the idea for the opening of *The Tempest*

- There has been much speculation about why the majority of Shakespeare's great tragedies were written one after the other in the years after 1600. Might this have been because of a deep melancholy which Shakespeare needed to release following the death of his son, Hamnet? Or was it, perhaps, because of the increasing disquiet in society which was eventually to lead to the English Civil War? Certainly, Shakespeare's contemporaries were predominantly writing about such subjects as intrigue, deception, murder and other black deeds

- Shakespeare's final four plays – *Pericles, Cymbeline, A Winter's Tale* and *The Tempest* – are sometimes described as "the plays of reconciliation and hope". They seem to show us a man who has come to terms with tragedy and is able at last to feel peace. It is interesting to speculate on why this came about

Also students should look at Shakespeare's "farewell to the stage" which is said to occur in Prospero's final speech in *The Tempest* where he says he will "break his staff" and "burn his books." This rounds off Shakespeare's writing beautifully doesn't it? Unfortunately the ending of Shakespeare's career was not so neat, as he is known to have collaborated with Fletcher on *Henry VIII* after completing *The Tempest.*

With a little research, you will find many other interesting links between the plays, Shakespeare's life and the social and political history of England. This can of course prove a most satisfying link with history projects undertaken in school.

SHAKESPEARE'S EDUCATION

Shakespeare's education was crucial in forming the basis from which he wrote, although Ben Jonson later wrote that Shakespeare knew "little Latin and less Greek." Stratford Grammar School, which Shakespeare attended, is still standing – and is still a school! An interesting project can be devised on the subjects Elizabethan children were taught and the ways in which they were taught.

Where did Shakespeare get his ideas for the plays? Well, he wasn't exactly the greatest originator – in fact little of his work is strictly his own. Instead he used stories and historical sources which would have been introduced to him at school – in particular Holinshed's *Chronicles* and Petrarch's *Lives*. I'm sure students would enjoy researching these sources and reading the original stories on which many of the plays were based.

As an example of ways in which students might tie together study of specific plays with background historical study, let us consider *The Merchant of Venice*. Anyone considering the role of Shylock in this play would need to appreciate how the Jews were hated by the Elizabethans, who considered that they were effectively holding the nation to ransom with their money-lending and usury. At the same time, Jews were permitted very limited areas of operation, one of which was money-lending. Christians were forbidden by the Pope to lend money and thereby accrue interest.

If we look at the strong roles that Shakespeare gave many of his female characters (such as Lady Macbeth, Cleopatra, Rosalind, Viola and Queen Margaret), we begin to see a picture of a man who seemed to respect women. Perhaps he was surrounded by strong women in his own life – what do we know about his mother and his wife?

Here consideration may also be given to the boy actors of the Elizabethan Theatre.

BOY-ACTORS

As no women were allowed to perform on the Elizabethan stage, we must consider that young boy-actors would have been expected to play most of the female roles. There is evidence, however, that some adult actors specialised in playing female roles, too, and it is unlikely that a twelve or thirteen year old would have tackled tragic heroines like Cleopatra and Lady Macbeth, or older characters like Queen Margaret, Constance and Gertrude. The boy-actors were brought up in the acting profession, often coming from a family where their father, brother or uncle was an actor too. Even so, this must have been an exacting task for them. If you are working with a group of boys, why not let them try some of the female roles themselves and see how they fare? It would also be helpful to research into the Boy Companies of actors who were in direct competition to the adult companies at this time. In *Hamlet*, these are referred to as "an eyrie of children, little eyases, that cry out on the top of question, and are most tyrranically clapp'd for it". Do you think modern audiences would go to see a play performed entirely by boys? How have our expectations changed with regard to realism in the theatre today?

I have suggested looking into the personal background of Shakespeare and this can provide some interesting ideas for further study.

ROLE-PLAY

Students may find it useful to improvise role-play situations which illustrate key moments in Shakespeare's life: for example, there is a widely-held belief that Shakespeare was forced to marry Anne Hathaway because she was pregnant. She was also three or four years his senior. How do you think he, and his family, might have reacted to a potentially illegitimate child?

Another example: nobody really knows what, if anything, happened to make him leave Stratford. Was it simply his ambition to make his mark in the theatre? A reluctance to follow in his father's footsteps and become a glove-maker?

And what about the so-called "lost years"? Perhaps your students could speculate on where he was and what he was doing. The research might take the form of a detective story with clues leading to possible conclusions. You could even present it as a Sherlock Holmes story with the great man himself and his trusted friend Dr. Watson attempting to solve "The Mystery of The Bard of Avon!"

SOCIAL AND POLITICAL BACKGROUND

By learning about Elizabethan life in general, students may begin to understand the way Shakespeare mirrored the political and social times in which he lived. He would include references to events and people which would be readily understood by his audience. By doing this, he brought the "groundlings" into the action and made them feel part of the play. It also gives us, as modern detectives, clues to the political opinions and news of the age. These were exciting, adventurous times. The Elizabethan court was a vibrant place, where a renaissance in art and literature was encouraged by a monarch who frequently requested performances at court by Shakespeare's company and their contemporaries. Great expeditions of discovery were undertaken by Raleigh and Drake; the Earl of Essex was fighting the Irish rebels; the Spanish Armada was defeated off Plymouth Hoe; Elizabeth I and James I alike inspired patriotism in their subjects. With these pointers we can search out events in the plays which would have been very meaningful to Elizabethan audiences.

For example, towards the end of her reign, Elizabeth was highly sensitive to anything concerned with the deposition of a rightful monarch. Shakespeare's *Richard II*, written in the early 1590s, was rarely performed – and when it *was* performed, the famous scene in which Richard gives up the crown to the usurper, Bolingbroke, was omitted. The Earl of Essex, Elizabeth's former favourite, raised a rebellion in London against her. The day before the rebellion (which folded within hours), an associate of Essex commissioned the Lord Chamberlain's men to perform the play, including the offending scene. Shakespeare and his leading actor, Burbage, were lucky to escape prison.

Royal patronage was extremely important at this time. It is difficult to comprehend today how much the arts were influenced by the Court during the Elizabethan age. The Queen was responsible for leading the tastes of the wealthy courtiers. Her approval, and later that of James I, were vital to any dramatist. Groups of actors were brought in to entertain the court with leading courtiers as their patrons. Indeed, if a troupe of players had no patron they were, in law, regarded as 'rogues and vagabonds' who could be locked up without charge. Shakespeare's company became the Lord Chamberlain's Men and began to perform at court. While the theatres were closed between 1592 and 1594, in an attempt to stop the spread of bubonic plague, plays would have been presented in the homes of the wealthy and, of course, for the Queen at Windsor. We know that Queen Elizabeth had favourite characters in Shakespeare's plays. After the death of Falstaff in *Henry V*, Elizabeth asked to see the character again in a comedy. As a result, Shakespeare wrote *The Merry Wives of Windsor*. This shows how successful Shakespeare had become by 1600.

In the reign of James I, Shakespeare wrote *Macbeth* because the new King was a distant descendant of Banquo, and also because of James' well-known interest in witchcraft and demonology.

We know that the Earl of Southampton was a particular friend of Shakespeare's. In fact there seems to have been a quite passionate friendship, which shows itself in some of the sonnets. These were dedicated to "the only known begetter, Mr WH". Southampton's name was Henry Wriothesley and the reversal of these initials is said to be a deliberate clue to

Southampton's identity. There have been other candidates for *Mr WH* over the years (including a delightful fantasy by Oscar Wilde) but Southampton remains the favourite candidate as the recipient of the sonnets. The sonnets also feature a mysterious 'Dark Lady,' whose identity has also been the cause of much speculation. Students might try to analyse these deeply personal poems and consider the identity of the recipients.

SONNET 78

So oft have I invok'd thee for my Muse,
And found such fair assistance in my verse
As every alien pen hath got my use,
And under thee their poesy disperse.
Thine eyes, that taught the dumb on high to sing
And heavy ignorance aloft to fly,
Have added feathers to the learnèd's wing,
And given grace a double majesty.
Yet be most proud of that which I compile,
Whose influence is thine, and born of thee:
In others' works thou dost but mend the style,
And arts with thy sweet graces gracèd be;
But thou art all my art, and dost advance
As high as learning my rude ignorance.

Following the death of Elizabeth in 1603 and the accession of James I, Shakespeare's company became The King's Men and unquestionably the top troupe of actors in London. However, Elizabeth's independent courtiers were replaced by flamboyant cavaliers and court life became increasingly artificial. Plays began to cater for the aristocracy. Under Elizabeth there had been a measure of religious tolerance, despite strong anti-Catholic feeling after the defeat of the Spanish Armada in 1588. James was nominally Protestant, but the family had been Catholic in the past, which bred suspicion. There was a growing number of hard-line Puritans who were bitterly hostile towards the theatre. Shakespeare is thought to have been Protestant by religion but in his writing he shows quite diverse opinions on religious belief.

I hope this section will encourage you to delve more deeply into the background of Shakespeare's life and the social history of his times. This can be linked into studies in the National Curriculum including science, culture, court life and religion. Above all, it will help to bring much greater understanding of the plays and their content.

BOOK LIST

Shakespeare in his Time, Ivor Brown, (Thomas Nelson & Sons)
Shakespeare and his World, F. E. Halliday, (Thomas Hudson Ltd)
Shakespeare the Man, A. L. Rowse, (Macmillan)
Shakespeare the Man, Geoffrey Ashton, (Studio Editions, London)
Introducing Shakespeare, G. B. Harrison, (Pelican Books)
The Elizabethan World Picture, E.M.W. Tillyard, (Penguin)

ELIZABETHAN THEATRE

Here's a marvellous convenient place for our rehearsal

A Midsummer Night's Dream Act I, Sc i

Students who have only been to their local theatre to see a pantomime once a year will find it very hard to appreciate what it must have been like to see a Shakespeare play in its original setting. It is very important that acting students should understand not only the structure of the building but the way in which this structure affected the manner of acting.

Begin by going back in history to see how drama was presented before this period. It is no coincidence that the interior of the first permanent theatres in England resembled very closely the inner courtyard of an inn – with an open space at the centre and balconies surrounding it. It would be very helpful if a model of the Elizabethan theatre could be constructed for use in class. There are several excellent commercial ones available – or why not design your own using simple materials.

THEATRE CONSTRUCTION

We are not absolutely certain about the way the theatres were constructed but some contemporary illustrations together with eye-witness descriptions give us a pretty good idea.

References within the plays talk about "this wooden O" (*Henry V*) which give us a rough exterior shape, although some were polygonal. The wooden stage – "this unworthy scaffold" – jutted out into the audience and stood between three and four feet high. The theatres were very large arenas, seating two to three thousand people. The audience was made up of all classes, trades and professions. It is interesting for students to note that the theatres were all built on the South Bank of the Thames which was outside the jurisdiction of the City of London – why was this necessary? Your students could find out.

This century some theatres have returned to the Elizabethan design and have managed to re-create something of the energy and strongly-charged relationship which existed because of the close proximity between audience and performer.

For anyone who lives in the Midlands, the Swan Theatre at Stratford-upon-Avon comes close to creating this atmosphere. It has a much smaller auditorium than the originals would have had but the audience are able to experience much the same excitement that Elizabethan audiences would have felt in being close to the action. This theatre is a modern, indoor structure and therefore cannot reproduce the open-air features of the Globe. Until now, this ultimate experience has been beyond our reach.

Now the new Globe Theatre, close to the original Bankside site, has been completed. This exciting project, brought to reality by the passionate determination of Sam Wanamaker, will enable students to see Shakespeare's plays presented in something close to their original setting. Summer workshops were held in 1995 to enable actors to try out the acoustics. Modern performers will need to radically change their delivery for this type of performance. Remember that actors will be competing with the surrounding noise of traffic, aircraft and the daily sounds of a bustling capital. I would urge students to make it an essential part of their training to see at least one production at the new Globe. Information may be obtained from Shakespeare's Globe, Bear Gardens, London SE1 9ED.

You might also find the video *The Life and Times of William Shakespeare* by Channel AV Television Ltd useful as it contains film showing the early stages of the Globe's construction as well as many other interesting insights into Shakespeare's history. The video is not readily available but you can obtain it from the Shakespeare Bookshop in Stratford-upon-Avon. Details can be found at the end of this book.

In 1995 the Post Office produced an excellent set of five stamps illustrating some of the first theatres constructed in

England – The Rose 1592, The Swan 1595, The Globe 1599 and The Hope 1613 with an additional picture of the second Globe rebuilt after the first burned down. Keep your eyes open for any similar material which can give your students visual stimulus and lead to further project work.

It is not my brief in this section to give an in-depth description of Elizabethan theatres. I want instead to give some practical ideas on how to research the subject.

PERFORMANCES

Why not begin by viewing the opening section of Laurence Olivier's 1940 film version of *Henry V*? This begins with a fascinating reconstruction of a performance being given in the Globe. We see the audience arriving and back-stage preparations in the tiring house (including the boy-actors dressing and props being collected). The whole of the first Act is then presented on stage showing us how the audience would have reacted to well-loved comedy stars and the leading actor. We can also see how entrances and exits were managed.

By studying the way in which Elizabethan actors worked, we can better understand some of the references within the text and the stage directions. For example, "within" refers to the use of a curtained-off section at the back of the stage and "above" to either a balcony which sometimes contained the musicians or a trap-door in the "heavens" (ceiling above part of the stage) through which gods could descend. This was a throw-back to medieval street theatre. The use of the upper chamber is referred to in *Antony and Cleopatra* Act IV scene xiii: "Enter Cleopatra and her Maides aloft." We can also find in *The Merchant of Venice* Act II scene v the direction, "Enter Jessica above, in boy's clothes". Then, of course, there is the balcony scene in *Romeo and Juliet*.

Scenery was sparse and probably just suggested the scene. Frequently the spoken word within the text suggested the setting and atmosphere. The best way to discover more about the stage and scenery is to look at the stage directions and to work out the staging from these, together with textual references.

ACTING STYLE

We very often talk about the "style" of acting required for different periods of dramatic writing. This understanding of the way actors worked can help modern students to enhance their own performance. I am not suggesting that we should all declaim in the 'grand manner' – this would be unacceptable to a modern audience. However, if we ignore the style – and scale – of delivery needed for the text we lose a great deal.

Let us consider what we know about the way the plays were performed in the Elizabethan theatre. To reach an audience of two to three thousand the actor would have needed to project strongly with clear gesture and an awareness of talking to an audience on three sides. Shakespeare himself gives us his opinions on good acting style in Hamlet's words to the players:

> Speak the speech, I pray you, as I pronounced it to you, trippingly on the tongue; but if you mouth it, as many of your players do, I had as lief the town-crier spoke my lines. Nor do not saw the air too much with your hand, thus, but use all gently; for in the very torrent, tempest, and, as I may say, the whirlwind of passion, you must acquire and beget a temperance that may give it smoothness... Be not too tame neither, but let your own discretion be your tutor. Suit the action to the word, the word to the action; with this special observance, that you o'erstep not the modesty of nature; for anything so o'erdone is from the purpose of playing, whose end, both at the first and now, was and is to hold, as 't were, the mirror up to nature...

> *Hamlet*, Act III Sc iii

Shakespeare, then, had very strong opinions on how actors should perform. He favoured a naturalistic style within the conventions of the time. How did the members of his company rehearse a new play?

Well, in modern terms, they didn't! The actors performed a different play each day of the week and had as many as a hundred plays available at any one time. To enable them to do this, they worked from 'cue scripts' which contained only their own lines and a three word cue. They did not know who was going to deliver the cue line and therefore had to concentrate absolutely on the scene and on the information contained in their own lines. Shakespeare tells us a great deal about a character's emotional state and relationship with others in the lines themselves. Let us look at a cue-script for a minor character taken from the final scene of *Romeo and Juliet.*

Character: First Watch

1.	Cue:- lips are warm!
2.(*within*) Lead, boy: which way?	
3.	Cue:- let me die.
4.	Cue:- torch doth burn.
5.	The ground is bloody; search about the churchyard.
6.	Go, some of you; whoe'er you find, attach.
7.	Pitiful sight! Here lies the county slain,
8.	And Juliet bleeding, warm, and newly dead,
9.	Who here hath lain this two days buried.
10.	Go, tell the prince, run to the Capulets,
11.	Raise up the Montagues, some others search:
12.	We see the ground whereon these woes do lie;
13.	But the true ground of all these piteous woes
14.	We cannot without circumstance descry.
15.	Cue:- in the churchyard.
16.	Hold him in safety till the prince come hither.
17.	Cue:- this churchyard side.
18.	A great suspicion: stay the friar too.
19.	Cue:- in our ears?
20.	Sovereign, here lies the County Paris slain;
21.	And Romeo dead; and Juliet, dead before,
22.	Warm and new killed.
23.	Cue:- foul murder comes.

24.   Here is a friar, and slaughter'd Romeo's man,
25.   With instruments upon them fit to open
26.   These dead men's tombs.
27.   Cue:- and her Romeo
(*Exeunt*)

For ease of understanding I have numbered the lines to help you follow what the actor would ascertain on first view of his script. All the instructions he needs to play the First Watch are contained within the cue script.

Line 2: He speaks off stage and is about to enter.

The gap between lines 3 and 4: He enters but says nothing

Lines 5,6: The lines tell him that there are others with him over whom he has some authority.

Lines 7,8: The lines give him moves to where the bodies lie.

Lines 10,11: The lines show him that there are still members of the watch present who will exit at the end of the second line.

Line 16: Obviously some watchmen have returned with a prisoner (in fact it is Balthasar).

Line 18: The Friar has entered too.

Line 20: Now the Prince is on stage and the first watchman sets the scene for him. (In fact Capulet and Lady Capulet have also entered but are not yet central to the action).

Lines 24–26: He continues to point out the characters present and then moves to the background as other characters take the fore. He remains silent until the final exit after the last line of the play.

It is incredible to think how Elizabethan actors could produce such complex plays with hardly any rehearsal but they did. This is where students can have fun while learning to find the detail in the text that they would never normally see.

Produce cue-scripts for any scene with plenty of characters: perhaps *Antony and Cleopatra* Act II scene vii; *Julius Caesar* Act III scene i; or *The Taming of the Shrew* Act III scene ii. If you have lots of time to spend, the class could make up a cue script each for a different character and then swap them about so that they are unfamiliar with their part. Now try to act out the scene with only the essential information – setting and place in the story. I think you will be amazed at how much can be achieved in a first performance although there may also be quite a lot of hilarity as characters try to recognise their cues.

If you want to be authentic, the cue scripts should be on a single scroll. It is interesting to note that the part of Lady Macbeth would only extend to about half a metre. This brings a whole new meaning to the actor's concern about the length of his or her role!

Again we can find references in the text to the way Shakespeare's company worked. Apart from Hamlet's address to the players, which I have already mentioned, take a look at Act I scene ii of *A Midsummer Night's Dream* where the mechanicals meet for the first time to discuss their forthcoming production of *Pyramus and Thisbe*. Lines in the text suddenly take on more meaning:

> BOTTOM: Now, good Peter Quince, call forth
>   your actors by the scroll.
> SNUG: Have you the lion's part written? Pray
>   you, if it be, give it me, for I am slow of study.

If you find this aspect of Shakespeare as fascinating as I do, you might like to contact the Original Shakespeare Company who offer workshops in schools using the First Folio text and cue scripts. The address can be found at the end of the book.

BOOK LIST

Shakespeare's Theatre, Wendy Greenhill for the RSC, (Heinemann)
Elizabethan Theatre, David Birt, (Longman)

Shakespeare and his Theatre, Jim Bradbury, (Longman)

Shakespeare's Theatre, Jacqueline Morley & John James, (Simon & Schuster) (suitable for Juniors – colourful and explained simply)

Shakespeare and his Theatre, John Russell Brown, (Kestrel books) (could also be used by top Juniors)

The World of the Swan pamphlet, (RSC)

This Golden Round – the RSC at the Swan, Ronnie Mulryne & Margaret Shewring, (RSC)

This Wooden 'O': Shakespeare's Globe Reborn, Barry Day, (Oberon Books)

COSTUME

A silken doublet, a velvet hose,
a scarlet cloak

The Taming of the Shrew Act V Scene i

There has always been discussion about what actors should wear when performing Shakespeare. Many audiences are disappointed when they attend a production and find that the director has chosen to present it in modern dress. However, we must remember that Elizabethan actors wore contemporary clothes for their performances – which really means that they on the whole wore 'modern dress' too! So, does that mean that your teenage student, acting Juliet, can wear Dr Martens and a pair of jeans? No, of course it doesn't! The point about movement for Shakespeare in examinations is that it should have the correct style and poise to suit the character being presented. An understanding of Elizabethan costume can help a student to create a realistic performance within the context of the scene. This study can be effectively linked with art and history in schools. Let us look at the key factors which should be researched.

ELIZABETHAN DRESS

I do not intend to give detailed descriptions of costume here as there are many publications available, some of which I have listed at the end of this chapter. I want instead to look at what was worn by the actors on stage and what references we can find within the plays to dress.

We know that actors playing servants or poor characters would have simply worn their own clothes. For those playing rich, noble characters it was more difficult to create the fashionable effect required. The actors relied on the generosity of noble benefactors and supporters of the theatre, like the Earl of Southampton, who would give their 'old' clothes to the company. This enabled the leading players to look suitably grand – which seems to have been very important to Elizabethan audiences. There is evidence that companies were prepared to spend considerable amounts on 'costume', with less emphasis on the use of correct props and appropriate scenery which we would think important.

How then did Shakespeare's actors suggest the period of the Roman plays or the early Britain of Cymbeline? Well, they didn't really try too hard. In fact only some small suggestions of costume were needed. We do have a contemporary illustration of a performance of *Titus Andronicus* in 1594 which shows the leading actor wearing something resembling a Roman toga draped around his tunic and hose. Perhaps an actor might add a Roman helmet to his normal dress but generally the audience seem to have accepted contemporary clothes as the norm and the setting and period would have been described within the text. Imagination was everything!

As always Shakespeare tells us quite a lot in the text.

- Dogberry in *Much Ado About Nothing* considers himself to be a respectable and well-to-do man. He boasts 'and one, moreover, that hath two coats.'

- Polonius gives this advice to Laertes in Hamlet: 'Costly thy habit as thy purse can buy, / But not express'd in fancy; rich, not gaudy; / For the apparel oft proclaims the man.'

- In the same play, Hamlet's apparent madness is indicated by his dishevelled appearance, reported in Ophelia's speech: 'Lord Hamlet, with his doublet all unbrac'd, / No hat upon his head, his stockings foul'd, / Ungart'red, and down-gyved to his ankle...'

- Petruchio is being particularly awkward in *The Taming of the Shrew* when he gives us some clear tips for the fashionable Elizabethan lady: 'Thy gown? Why, ay. / Come, tailor, let us see't... / What's this? a sleeve? 'Tis like a demi-cannon. / What, up and down, carv'd like an apple-tart? / Here's snip and nip and cut and slish and slash...'

It is obviously important for the actor to know what he is describing here.

The Elizabethans were given quite specific information by the colour and style of costume worn. Maria describes how she has tricked Malvolio in *Twelfth Night*:

He will come to her in yellow stockings, and 'tis a colour she abhors, and cross-gart'red, a fashion she detests...'

Audiences then would know that yellow was a colour traditionally worn by lovers – which would have increased their amusement at the joke played on Malvolio.

Black would be worn to show sadness and mourning (as it still is today) but was also a symbol of the law and would have been worn by lawyers. Doctors wore red and women who went mad (Lady Macbeth and Ophelia, for example) were traditionally depicted with their hair long and unkempt.

MODERN ADAPTATION

What then can a student gain from a study of Elizabethan dress? There are a number of aspects of costume which can be simply adapted to enhance an examination performance. The posture of the body is extremely important. Even if you intend to present your character in modern dress you must hold the body upright with the head erect but not stiff. Shoulders should be relaxed to aid ease of gesture. If possible open out the gesture from the shoulders (rather than from the elbows which is a modern convention). Movement has purpose and motivation – you should not shuffle about in an aimless way.

You do not wear 'costume' as such for LAMDA examinations. However, you can help yourself achieve appropriate style by wearing soft, flexible shoes with small heels. Dancers have an advantage here as character shoes and some Greek sandals are ideal. Boots and heavy shoes should be avoided – unless chosen for a specific character – as they inhibit flexibility of movement. If you wish to present your character in period, female students will find a full-length A-line or circular skirt invaluable. It is surprising how much more elegant you feel with this suggestion of period. If playing Viola or Rosalind, a woman will find leggings ideal as they give the effect of hose. With a tunic top and belt you can really suggest the character.

Boys should wear trousers which do not restrict movement, so avoid tight jeans, and appropriate upper garments. Perhaps an open-necked shirt and waistcoat for a mechanical or young gallant; a jacket for an older character might be useful. Make sure that sleeves do not cover the hands. It is amazing how often gesture is lost under a mound of knitting! These ideas are by no means meant to be comprehensive. I simply want you to think about your dress and remember that it is a crucial part of your performance. Often students do not realise how much this matters. I recently saw Titania presented at a summer session wearing a pair of shorts and a tee-shirt (because the candidate was leaving for her holiday immediately afterwards!) It was very hard for me to believe in her characterisation and equally hard for her to convey the majesty and mystique of this character. A little forethought would have improved the experience for both of us.

Now we come to hair! It is amazing that girls still come to examinations with long hair dangling over their faces and fringes obscuring the eyes. You must remember that your eyes are vital in allowing the audience to see your emotion and sincerity. You should always fix the hair back so that it does not get in the way.

PROJECT WORK

The history of costume is a fascinating subject and one which easily fits into school subjects such as history, art, design and textiles. There are many excellent books available on the subject and students can draw or paint their own designs based on the Elizabethan period or create costume designs for an individual Shakespeare play. *A Midsummer Night's Dream* is of course a favourite starting point as the imagination can really go to town on the supernatural characters.

Remember, however, that three dimensions are always better than two. A visit to one of the excellent costume museums will give a much clearer idea of how shape and weight of fabric can affect movement for the actor. Unfortunately, very little actual Elizabethan clothing has survived the passage of time but the tight corseting can be appreciated in later styles and you will find some examples of bodices and underwear on view. I particularly recommend the costume department of the Victoria and Albert Museum in London and the Museum of Costume in Bath.

However, if you cannot arrange a trip to a museum, why not let your students make their own costume model? Making up the separate sections of the dress will help them to understand the detailed structure of Elizabethan costume.

This is great fun to do and I'm sure many of you could design a male equivalent to show doublet and hose. After making a model why not try a full size costume? This is not as difficult as you might imagine. I have found the illustrations in *Spotlight on Shakespeare* (listed at the end of this section) particularly good. They include instructions for creating an Elizabethan male and female costume as well as ideas for characters in *A Midsummer Night's Dream.*

Do remember that Gold Medal Verse and Prose students are expected to have an in-depth understanding of the costume of their Shakespeare character. Often answers are very sketchy indeed. I would suggest that making a model like this – or at least doing a design on paper – would show that you had done your research and would enable you to discuss the costume with ease.

There are a number of commercially available costume dolls which teachers might like to consider as aids to their class work. Relatively inexpensive ones are made by Peggy

Nesbet Ltd (available in tourist shops in Stratford, London etc) and by Teresa Thompson of 35, Lonsdale Way, Oakham, Leics LE15 6LP.

In addition to dolls, students might like to collect postcards of paintings of the time which often give very helpful representations of court dress. Keep your eyes open for these at art galleries, museums and stately homes. As these are cheap, you can readily collect a selection which will give you plenty of information about the designs and styles available to the nobility in Shakespeare's time. I have also managed to find quite a number of stamps which illustrate historical costume. Shops and mail-order philatelic organisations will select stamps on the theme of costume for you if you are interested.

I hope this information will have given you some ideas on how to make costume and movement an integral part of your Shakespeare study.

BOOK LIST

The Anatomy of Costume, Robert Selbie, (Mills & Boon)

High Fashion in Shakespeare's Time, Andrew Brownfoot, (Tarquin Publications)

Making Historical Costume Dolls, Jack Cassin-Scott, (Batsford Ltd)

English Costume in the Age of Elizabeth, Iris Brooke, (A&C Black Ltd)

Clothes in History, Charlotte Sewell, (Wayland)

Clothes for Work, Play & Display, Jacqueline Morley, (Watts)

Costume Through the Ages, Ella Bruce, (The Medici Society) (Suitable for Juniors)

Spotlight on Shakespeare, Sandy Brownjohn & Gareth Gwyn-Jones, (Hodder & Stoughton) (Also suitable for Juniors)

STRUCTURE AND SPEECH

The elegancy, facility, and golden cadence of poesy...

Love's Labour's Lost Act IV Sc ii

WHAT IS BLANK VERSE?

This question often opens the discussion on theory for a
student of Shakespeare and the simplest reply is "unrhyming
iambic pentameter". However it is not really sufficient for the
answer to be a "parrot fashion" definition. It is quite daunting
for a class of 12 year olds to be faced with "iambic pentameter",
something which sounds extremely difficult to understand; so
I would suggest that you begin by exploring poetic rhythm in
general.

How often examiners find that a student knows what
iambic metre is but doesn't realise that this is only one of a
number of rhythms which can be found in verse. This is
extremely important as Shakespeare did not write
exclusively in iambics.

Let us then begin with the origins of English prosody
which takes us back to Ancient Greece. The terms which we
use today to denote the different rhythms in verse are derived
from Greek or Latin words. "Rhythm", "Prose" and "Verse"
are Latin words, with "Metre" being a Greek word meaning
"measure". We "measure" the rhythm in a line of verse by the
number of stresses we find in it and by the repeated groups
of syllables which create that rhythm – these are called "feet".

As an analogy, I suggest you compare a line of verse with
a line of music:-

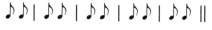

= 2 beats in a bar

In iambic pentameter, there are five feet in a verse line,
each foot consisting of two syllables. The IAMBIC stress

pattern is light/heavy. If we take Macbeth's line, 'But wherefore could I not pronounce Amen?', the iambic stresses give the line the following shape ('o' represents a light stress and '−' a heavy stress):

o   −   o   −   o −   o   −   o   −

But where | fore could | I not | pronounce | Amen? ||

If we reverse this rhythm and put the stress on the first syllable we have a TROCHAIC rhythm.

−   o   −   o   −   o   −   o

If we | spirits | have of | fended ||

This example is TROCHAIC TETRAMETER because there are only four feet in the line.

You should also mention the two triple rhythms:

DACTYLIC: one heavy stress followed by two light stresses

−   o   o

"Dactylic" derives from a Greek word meaning "finger" and describes the appropriate shape – one long joint followed by two short ones.

−   o   o

"Cookery" is a naturally dactylic word.

ANAPAESTIC: two light stresses followed by one heavy stress

o   o   −

o   o   −

The word "anapaest" itself has an anapaestic rhythm.

This basic information should make it easier for students to understand that Shakespeare was following the blank verse tradition of other writers of his time and earlier. The iambic pentameter is the verse form which is closest to the rhythms of English speech: 'I'm going to the pub to have a pint', for example, is a perfect line of iambic pentameter. In other languages, other verse forms most appropriately fit the language rhythms. Both the Greeks and the French, for example, use the hexameter (six feet).

Students should understand *why* Shakespeare wrote as he did. He did not, after all, "invent" this rhythm himself. What he did was "adapt" what had been a quite rigid form to something which allowed his actors freedom and expression within the lines.

Shakespeare would have read the iambic rhythm in the sonnets of writers like Henry Howard, Earl of Surrey, while he was still at school. The sonnet form – fourteen lines of iambic pentameter – would later be used by Shakespeare in some of his plays as well as in his sonnet sequences. Contemporaries like Christopher Marlowe used the iambic rhythm in their plays but it was quite rigid in form and frequently rhyming.

We can look at the plays themselves for clues as to how Shakespeare developed iambic pentameter into the blank verse which has helped his plays to stand the test of time. As I have pointed out on a number of occasions, students should look for the information they need within the text which they are studying. So much information is contained here if they can only discover it.

Let us glance through the plays from 1590 to 1613 to see how the iambic pentameter changes.

In the early plays, for example *Henry VI*, the iambic pentameter is fairly rigid, with quite a lot of rhyme and lines frequently end-stopped (the sense ending at the line ending). During the "development" stage of Shakespeare's writing, around 1595/96, we find *A Midsummer Night's Dream*. By this time, enjambment is being used to continue the sense into the next line. This immediately gives the verse a more natural flow.

For example, Helena Act I Sc i ll 246-9

> I will go tell him of fair Hermia's flight;
> Then to the wood will he tomorrow night
> Pursue her; and for this intelligence
> If I have thanks, it is a dear expense.

You will also find whole speeches in rhyming couplets.

The later tragedies and mystical plays show the greatest variation in the iambic pentameter. The blank verse is developed into a very natural form, which makes it ideal for the actor. Lots of variations in the rhythmical pattern are introduced, including substitutions of a trochaic foot; a pyrrhic (two unstressed beats); a spondee (two stressed beats) and a metrical pause (omissions of a syllable or foot). This development of the iambic pentameter is what marks Shakespeare out from his contemporaries.

Now we understand what blank verse is. Was this the only form of writing Shakespeare used in his plays? No, it certainly wasn't – although students are not always aware of this fact.

Shakespeare used all of the four main poetic rhythms as well as rhyming couplets and prose. Even in the later plays, where rhyme is rarely used, a rhyming couplet may still finish off a scene. This was an important aural cue to the audience that one piece of action was coming to an end and another was about to begin.

Let us consider how *A Midsummer Night's Dream* is constructed. The opening scene is written in blank verse as befits the dignity of Duke Theseus' court. The dialogue becomes rhyming couplets when Helena, Hermia and Lysander are left alone. Next we meet the mechanicals at Peter Quince's house. The whole scene is spoken in prose, showing the audience that these are comic characters and of a lower class. The opening of Act II introduces the fairies with a fascinating speech which begins with anapaests and then moves into trochees. This powerful rhythm introduces us to characters who are obviously different to those that we have already met. The entrance of the Fairy Queen Titania gives Shakespeare the chance to write the most beautiful blank verse in the play. Look at the imagery and language used in the speech beginning "These are the forgeries of jealousy."

In Act II scene ii the fairy song "You Spotted Snakes" is written in trochees and Oberon casts his spell on Titania in rhyming couplets of trochaic tetrameter. The following short dialogue between Lysander and Hermia is conducted in rhyming couplets of iambic pentameter.

We can see a pattern of language and form developing. Titania speaks in powerfully-written blank verse. The lovers speak in iambic pentameter which often rhymes. The fairies, particularly Puck, have their own special rhythm – the trochaic foot. Finally, the comic mechanicals speak in prose. This information can help the actor to create his or her character, understanding his position in the play and his relationship with the other characters.

These are very broad guidelines, of course. Puck *does* speak iambic pentameter on occasion, as does Oberon, and the mechanicals speak verse but only the strict rhythmic doggerel verse used for the play within a play, *Pyramus and Thisbe.* These changes are very important for the actor. We are being told to note a change of direction or emotion for this speech or scene. Remember that Elizabethan actors gleaned as much as they could from the text and modern students often miss this rich underlying thread of information.

When a student is preparing a speech for an examination, he or she should look at the character's progress through the play. Take note of any changes in the form of the speeches and remember that Shakespeare is giving information about that character. Let's look at some of the variations that occur and try to find reasons for them:

The Merchant Of Venice

- Shylock speaks prose when plotting against his Christian foes. We would have expected this major character to speak verse as he does elsewhere in the play, but because the Jewish moneylenders were hated by the Elizabethans, theatre-goers would have jeered and derided him – hence the prose, suggesting a low status

- Portia speaks verse except in some scenes with Nerissa: for example Act I scene ii. This is a personal conversation between two friends in which they discuss and make fun of some of Portia's suitors. It is quite flippant in style and prose is therefore the most appropriate form. You can find examples of this in other plays – why not look for them?

Twelfth Night

The famous "Willow Cabin" scene, Act I scene v, between Viola and Olivia changes mid-way from prose to verse. We find here a scene which begins with a lack of interest from Olivia and a general feeling of witty banter. This changes dramatically when Viola begins to deliver her prepared speech and Olivia instantly falls in love!

Romeo and Juliet

The Nurse alternates between verse and prose. See Act I scene iii, as she remembers her own dead child and Juliet's childhood, for an example of verse and the end of Act II scene iv for a scene in which she teases Romeo in prose. This colourful character moves from bawdy banter to tender reminiscence. The different aspects of her character are reflected in the style of the words she speaks.

King Lear

The Fool speaks verse. This appears at first sight to be a real puzzle. All the other clowns (Feste in *Twelfth Night*, the clowns in *Hamlet*) speak prose. The point Shakespeare is making here is that this fool is a wise man who supports Lear in his time of trial.

Othello

Iago speaks his scenes with Roderigo and Cassio in prose. Iago presents himself as a bluff soldier, a man's man. This directness and apparent honesty is mirrored in straightforward, less formally structured language. When Iago is alone, his great soliloquys of evil are in blank verse.

Othello's rich blank verse breaks down totally when he kills Desdemona. Act V scene ii: "Oh, Desdemona! Desdemona! Dead! Oh! Oh! Oh!"

This signals the moment that Othello's sense of himself as a noble being finally breaks down, though he gathers himself sufficiently to deliver his death speech in verse.

You can find many more examples if you look for them.

There is an unusually high proportion of prose in *Much Ado About Nothing, The Merry Wives of Windsor* and *As You Like It.* Find out why.

To help students feel at ease speaking iambic pentameter, divide them into pairs and help them to invent their own conversation in modern blank verse. For example:

Student A: If only I could get to Bob's tonight.

Student B: We thought we saw him going to the pub.

Or something similar!

Remember that familiarity with the rhythm will help take away the mystique of Shakespeare's language.

Another interesting exercise is to take a speech written in blank verse and write it down without the lines or punctuation. Now, in pairs or small groups, students can try to write it in its original form.

You may like to try this extract from *Julius Caesar* Act III scene ii:

if you have tears prepare to shed them now you all
do know this mantle I remember the first time ever
Caesar put it on twas on a summers evening in his

tent that day he overcame the Nervii look in this place ran Cassius dagger through see what a rent the envious Casca made through this the well beloved Brutus stabbd and as he pluckd his cursed steel away mark how the blood of Caesar followed it as rushing out of doors to be resolved if Brutus so unkindly knockd or no for Brutus as you know was Caesars angel judge o you gods how dearly Caesar loved him this was the most unkindest cut of all for when the noble Caesar saw him stab ingratitude more strong than traitors arms quite vanquished him then burst his mighty heart and in his mantle muffling up his face even at the base of Pompeys statua which all the while ran blood great Caesar fell o what a fall was there my countrymen then I and you and all of us fell down whilst bloody reason flourished over us o now you weep and I perceive you feel the dint of pity these are gracious drops kind souls what weep you when you but behold our Caesars vesture wounded look you here here is himself marrd as you see with traitors.

Many people will tell you that they were put off Shakespeare at an early age by being made to read a play "round the class". This expressionless, cold reading of the words, which are often not understood, is the best way to destroy a love of Shakespeare. I would urge teachers *always* to let students *act out* the scenes they are studying. Don't worry if you only have a classroom full of desks with little space to move in. There is *always* enough for standing up and a little movement and you could perhaps incorporate the desks as part of the setting – or move them, if this is possible.

We have talked about using the stories in modern translation to introduce the plays to younger students. To help older students understand the verse, you may wish to start with the more accessible sections of plays presented in a form which will appeal to them. An interesting recent publication by Paul Nimmo contains two short plays which include many famous speeches and scenes from *Hamlet,*

Romeo and Juliet, Julius Caesar, A Midsummer Night's Dream, The Tempest, Henry V, As You Like It, Twelfth Night, Much Ado About Nothing, Richard III and *Henry IV Part I.* The plays, which are entitled *Will Shakespeare Save Us!* and *Will Shakespeare Save The King!* use the idea of a bored King and his Chamberlain who become involved with a group of Players. The extracts from the plays are linked by modern conversations and it is possible to use the plays separately or to put them together for a full evening's production. In class you can choose sections to work on which concentrate on specific plays.

If you are studying *Hamlet,* your students would thoroughly enjoy *The Fifteen Minute Hamlet* by Tom Stoppard. Stoppard has very cleverly taken the key lines from the play and put them together to make a perfectly sensible interpretation of the story which is extremely funny. It plays at a frantic pace and considerable amusement can be had by looking for what has been omitted. For example, the most famous soliloquy in the play is reduced to one line! You can use a maximum of 16 actors or a minimum of six for guaranteed chaos!

Let us re-cap with a few thoughts on how to speak blank verse:

- Use the punctuation – remember that observing the full-stops and commas will make the words make sense

- TAKE YOUR TIME! Please PAUSE and THINK

- Translate your speech into modern English so that you know *exactly* what you are saying

- Remember that "ed" at the end of a word is often pronounced as a separate syllable. You should be able to hear this in the rhythm of the line

USING YOUR VOICE

The voice is a dynamic instrument. To play it well and to achieve the best results you must exercise it and carefully nurture it. These guidelines apply whether you are speaking poetry, reading aloud or acting. However, there is an extra element involved when acting Shakespeare – STYLE.

In the days of the Victorian actor-manager, Shakespeare was often "orated" in a grand manner with exaggerated emphasis and large gestures. Nowadays audiences demand a more naturalistic approach. However, it is important to bring the voice forward on the breath, paying particular attention to projection and rounded vowel sounds. Make your voice work together with your facial expression, gesture and movement to bring your character to life. If you are playing Hamlet or Cleopatra it is obviously important that you speak good Standard English. Remember that any hint of a local accent will stop the characterisation from being truthful. You can, however, use more licence with comic characters who might benefit from a dialect to give them added colour. Characters who come under this heading might include Phebe and Sylvius in *As You Like It*, Launce in *The Two Gentlemen of Verona*, the Nurse in *Romeo and Juliet*, the mechanicals in *A Midsummer Night's Dream*, the Watch in *Much Ado About Nothing* and Mistress Quickly in *The Merry Wives of Windsor*. This is not a definitive list. Explore the plays and find others for yourself.

I do not intend to give general voice exercises as there are many excellent publications available to help you in this area. A general physical and vocal warm-up should always proceed any practical work on Shakespeare. If you prepare well you will achieve the results you want.

BOOK LIST

The Fifteen Minute Hamlet, Tom Stoppard, (Samuel French Ltd)

Will Shakespeare Save Us! / Will Shakespeare Save The King!, Paul Nimmo, (Dramatic Lines)

Teaching Shakespeare, Peter Reynolds, (Oxford University Press)

The Making of Verse, Swann & Sidgwick, (Sidgwick & Jackson Ltd)

Voice and Speech in the Theatre, J. Clifford Turner, (Pitman & Sons Ltd)

Clear Speech, Malcolm Morrison, (Pitman)

Voice Production and Speech, Greta Colson, (Museum Press)

The Voice Book, Michael McCallian, (Faber & Faber)

Voice and the Actor, Cicely Berry, (Harrap)

PROJECTS

A MIDSUMMER NIGHT'S DREAM (1595-6)

I know a bank whereon the wild thyme blows

Act II Scene i

Suggested age-group: Junior/Lower Senior
Access: Stories in modern English
     Film - *The Animated Tales*
Music: *Sabre-Dance* by Khachaturian
     The Carnival of The Animals by Saint Saens
     Your choice of music for *You Spotted Snakes*
     (Also Mendelssohn's music for the play)
Props: Animal Masks

Refer back to "Beginnings" for ideas on costume and setting. I have adapted a script using Act II scene i, Act III scene i and the Epilogue to make a short playlet for classroom use. You have 14 characters to explore the supernatural elements in the play.

Begin by working on the dance-drama part of the scene. The *Sabre-Dance* or any other similar music which gives a great deal of energy through strong rhythm can be used. Play the piece to the children and let them find an individual style of movement for each of the ten fairies. These then enter separately to a section of the music before finally joining together for a last chaotic climax. Explore the relationships within the group here. Perhaps some of the fairies are "show offs"; others may be antagonistic, shy or cheeky. Encourage the children to make their movements different from everyone else and to use the music as stimulus to help them create their characters.

The other dance-drama sequence involves the use of animal masks which can be made beforehand by the children if commercially made ones are not available. Some initial work on animal movement should be done before proceeding to the music to be used – *The Carnival of the Animals*. You can find a wealth of good material here, but I would particularly recommend the braying of a donkey which can signal the entrance of Bottom complete with ass's head! The animals can show inquisitiveness at this strange being, followed by starting in fear at his movements before a rapid exit.

Bottom can invent a tune for his short song and the class can learn "You Spotted Snakes" before adding the music to it, then leading Titania to her bower and covering her with leaves. You now have all the elements you need to put the whole scene together with the script.

FAIRY DANCE

FAIRY 1:   Over hill, over dale,
           Thorough bush, thorough brier,

FAIRY 2:   Over park, over pale,
           Thorough flood, thorough fire,

FAIRY 3:   I do wander everywhere,
           Swifter than the moon's sphere;

FAIRY 4:   And I serve the Fairy Queen,
           To dew her orbs upon the green.

FAIRY 5:   The cowslips tall her pensioners be;
           In their gold coats spots you see;

FAIRY 6:   Those be rubies, fairy favours,
           In those freckles live their savours.

FAIRY 7:   I must go seek some dewdrops here
           And hang a pearl in every cowslip's ear.

FAIRY 8:   Farewell, thou lob of spirits; I'll be gone,
           Our Queen and all her elves come here anon.

FAIRY 9:   Either I mistake your shape and making quite,
           Or else you are that shrewd and navish sprite
           Called Robin Goodfellow.

PUCK: Thou speakest aright:
I am that merry wanderer of the night.
I jest to Oberon, and make him smile
When I a fat and bean-fed horse beguile,
Neighing in likeness of a filly foal.
But room, fairy, here comes Oberon.

FAIRY 10:   And here my mistress. Would that he were gone!

TITANIA: Come now, a roundel and a fairy song;
Sing me now asleep;
Then to your offices, and let me rest.

FAIRY SONG

You spotted snakes with double tongue,
Thorny hedgehogs, be not seen;
Newts and blindworms, do no wrong,
Come not near our fairy Queen.

Philomel with melody
Sing in our sweet lullaby.
Lulla, lulla, lullaby; lulla, lulla, lullaby.
Never harm
Nor spell nor charm
Come our lovely lady nigh.
So good night, with lullaby.

Weaving spiders come not here;
Hence, you long-legg'd spinners, hence.
Beetles black, approach not near;
Worm nor snail do no offence.

Philomel with melody
Sing in our sweet lullaby.
Lulla, lulla, lullaby; lulla, lulla, lullaby.
Never harm
Nor spell nor charm
Come our lovely lady nigh.
So good night, with lullaby.

FAIRY: Hence away; now all is well.
One aloof stand sentinel.

OBERON smears the juice on Titania's eyes

OBERON: What thou seest when thou dost wake,
Do it for thy true-love take;
Be it ounce, or cat, or bear,
Pard, or boar with bristled hair,
When thou wak'st, it is thy dear.
Wake when some vile thing is near.

OBERON exits

FAIRY DANCE (Animal Masks)

BOTTOM: Why do they run away? This a knavery of them to make me afeard. This is to make an ass of me; to fright me, if they could. But I will not stir from this place, do what they can; I will walk up and down here, and I will sing, that they shall hear I am not afraid.

The ousel cock, so black of hue,
With orange-tawny bill
The throstle with his note so true,
The wren with little quill.

TITANIA: What angel wakes me from my flow'ry bed?
I pray thee, gentle mortal, sing again.
For on the first view I must say I love thee.

BOTTOM: Methinks, mistress, you should have little reason for that.

TITANIA: Thou art as wise as thou art beautiful.

BOTTOM: Not so, neither; but if I had wit enough to get out of this wood, I would.

TITANIA: Out of this wood do not desire to go,
Though shalt remain here whether thou wilt
     or no.
I am a spirit of no common rate;
The summer still doth tend upon my state;
And I do love thee; therefore go with me.
I'll give thee fairies to attend on thee;
Peaseblossom! Cobweb! Moth! and
Mustardseed!

FAIRIES: Ready.
            And I.
            And I.
            And I.
            Where shall we go?

TITANIA: Be kind and courteous to this gentleman;
            Hop in his walks and gambol in his eyes;
            Feed him with apricots and dewberries,
            With purple grapes, green figs, and mulberries.
            Nod to him elves and do him courtesies.

FAIRIES: Hail mortal!
            Hail!
            Hail!
            Hail!

BOTTOM: I cry your worships mercy, heartily; I be-
            seech your worship's name.

FAIRY: Cobweb.

BOTTOM: I shall desire you of more acquaintance, good
            Master Cobweb. Your name, honest gentle-
            man?

FAIRY: Peaseblossom

BOTTOM: Good Master Peaseblossom, I shall desire you
            of more acquaintance too. Your name, I
            beseech you, sir?

FAIRY: Mustardseed

BOTTOM: Good Master Mustardseed, I promise you your
            kindred hath made my eyes water ere now.

TITANIA: Come, wait upon him; Lead him to my bower.

PUCK: If we shadows have offended,
            Think but this, and all is mended,
            That you have but slumb'red here
            While these visions did appear.
            And this weak and idle theme,
            No more yielding but a dream.
            Gentles' do not reprehend.

If you pardon, we will mend.
And, as I am an honest Puck,
If we have unearned luck
Now to 'scape the serpent's tongue,
We will make amends ere long;
Else the Puck a liar call.
So, good night unto you all.
Give me your hands, if we be friends,
And Robin shall restore amends.

Remember to encourage individual characterisation in speech and movement and above all an enjoyment of the performance. You may wish to incorporate more music (perhaps the Mendelssohn) into the scene. You can continue your work on the play with the *Pyramus and Thisbe* scene from Act V.

THE MERCHANT OF VENICE (1595-7)

The quality of mercy is not strain'd

Act IV scene i

Suggested age-group: Top Junior/Lower and Middle Senior
Access: Stories in modern English
Props: A scroll, scales, knife and any courtroom
    paraphernalia you care to add

Set up your classroom as a modern courtroom with a judge (who represents the Duke); a jury (of 12 class members); Shylock on one side opposite Antonio (the merchant) on the other; the defence lawyer (Portia); the Clerk of the Court (Nerissa); and a witness box (for Bassanio).

I have adapted speeches from Act I scene iii, Act III scene i and Act IV scene i to make the following court case. Move your characters around the courtroom as required.

JUDGE: What? Is Antonio here?

ANTONIO: Ready, so please your grace.

JUDGE: Go one, and call the Jew into the court.

CLERK: He's ready at the door: he comes, my lord.

JUDGE: Make room, and let him stand before our face.

Enter SHYLOCK

SHYLOCK: I have possess'd your grace of what I purpose;
 And by our holy Sabbath I have sworn
 To have the due and forfeit of my bond.

BASSANIO:For thy three thousand ducats here is six.

SHYLOCK: If every ducat in six thousand ducats
 Were in six parts, and every part a ducat,
 I would not draw them; I would have my bond.

JUDGE: How shall thou hope for mercy, rendering none?

SHYLOCK: What judgement should I dread, doing no
  wrong?
 The pound of flesh, which I demand of him
 Is dearly bought; 'tis mine, and I will have it.
 If you deny me, fie upon your law!

JUDGE: Upon my power I may dismiss this court,
 Unless Bellario, a learned doctor,
 Whom I have sent for to determine this,
 Come here today.

CLERK: My lord, here stays without
 A messenger with letters from the doctor,
 New come from Padua.

JUDGE: Bring us the letters.

He reads

 This letter from Bellario doth commend
 A young and learned doctor to our court.
 Where is he?

CLERK: He attendeth here hard by,
 To know your answer, whether you'll admit him.

JUDGE: With all my heart:
Go give him courteous conduct to this place.
Meantime, the court shall hear Bellario's letter.

CLERK (*reads*): Your grace shall understand that at the receipt of your letter I am very sick; but, in the instant that your messenger came, was with me a young doctor of Rome. I acquainted him with the cause in controversy between the Jew and Antonio the merchant and he is furnished with my opinion. I never knew so young a body with so old a head. I leave him to your gracious acceptance.

PORTIA enters disguised as a lawyer

JUDGE: Give me your hand. Come you from old Bellario?

PORTIA: I did, my lord.

JUDGE: You are welcome, take your place.
Are you acquainted with the difference
That holds this present question in the court?

PORTIA: I am informed throughly of the cause.
Which is the merchant here, and which is the Jew?

JUDGE: Antonio and old Shylock, both stand forth.

PORTIA: Is your name Shylock?

SHYLOCK: Shylock is my name.

PORTIA: You stand within his danger, do you not?

ANTONIO: Ay, so he says.

PORTIA: Do you confess the bond?

ANTONIO: I do.

PORTIA: Then must the Jew be merciful.

SHYLOCK: On what compulsion must I? Tell me that.

PORTIA: The quality of mercy is not strain'd,
It droppeth as the gentle rain from heaven

Upon the place beneath: it is twice bless'd;
It blesseth him that gives and him that takes:
'Tis mightiest in the mightiest; it becomes
The throned monarch better than his crown;
But mercy is above this sceptred sway;
It is enthroned in the hearts of kings,
It is an attribute to God himself;
> Therefore Jew,
Though justice be thy plea, consider this,
That in the course of justice none of us
Should see salvation: we do pray for mercy,
And that same prayer doth teach us all to render
The deeds of mercy.

SHYLOCK: My deeds upon my head! I crave the law,
The penalty and forfeit of my bond.
Signior Antonio, many a time and oft
In the Rialto you have rated me
About my moneys and my usances:
Still have I born it with a patient shrug,
For sufferance is the badge of all our tribe.
You call me misbeliever, cut-throat dog,
And spit upon my Jewish gaberdine,
And all for use of that which is mine own.
Well then, it now appears you need my help:
Go to then; you come to me, and you say,
"Shylock, we would have moneys." You say so;
You, that did void your rheum upon my beard,
And foot me as you spurn a stranger cur
Over your threshold: moneys is your suit.
What should I say to you? Should I not say,
"Hath a dog money? Is it possible
A cur can lend three thousand ducats?" Or
Shall I bend low, and in a bondsman's key,
With bated breath, and whispering humbleness,
Say this:
"Fair sir, you spit on me on Wednesday last;
You spurn'd me such a day; another time

[handwritten margin note: cur = bad tempered dog.]

You call'd me dog; and for these courtesies
I'll lend you thus much moneys"?

PORTIA: Is he not able to discharge the money?

BASSANIO: Yes, here I tender it for him in the court,
Yea, twice the sum: if that will not suffice,
I will be bound to pay it ten times o'er,
On forfeit of my hands, my head, my heart.

PORTIA: It must not be. There is no power in Venice
Can alter a decree established.
I pray you let me look upon the bond.

SHYLOCK: Here't is, most reverend doctor; here it is.

PORTIA: Why, this bond is forfeit;
And lawfully by this the Jew may claim
A pound of flesh, to be by him cut off
Nearest the merchant's heart. Be merciful:
Take thrice thy money; bid me tear the bond.

SHYLOCK: When it is paid according to the tenour.
It doth appear you are a worthy judge;
You know the law, your exposition
Hath been most sound:
I stay here on my bond.

ANTONIO: Most heartily I do beseech the court
To give the judgement.

PORTIA: Why then, thus it is:
You must prepare your bosom for his knife.
Therefore lay bare your bosom.
Are there balance here to weigh
The flesh?

SHYLOCK: I have them ready.

PORTIA: Have by some surgeon, Shylock, on your charge,
To stop his wounds, lest he do bleed to death.

SHYLOCK: Is it so nominated in the bond?

PORTIA: It is not so express'd; but what of that?
  T'were good you do so much for charity.

SHYLOCK: I cannot find it: 'tis not in the bond.

PORTIA: You, merchant, have you anything to say?

ANTONIO: But little: I am arm'd and well prepared.
  Give me your hand Bassanio: fare you well!
  Grieve not that I am fallen to this for you;
  Repent but you that you shall lose your friend.

PORTIA: A pound of that same merchant's flesh is thine.
  The court awards it and the law doth give it.
  And you must cut this flesh from off his breast:
  The law allows it, and the court awards it.

SHYLOCK: Most learned judge! A sentence! Come, prepare!

PORTIA: Tarry a little: there is something else.
  This bond doth give thee here no jot of blood;
  The words expressly are "a pound of flesh";
  Take then thy bond, take thou thy pound of flesh;
  But, in the cutting it, if thou dost shed
  One drop of Christian blood, thy lands and goods
  Are, by the laws of Venice, confiscate
  Unto the state of Venice.

SHYLOCK: Is that the law?

PORTIA: Thyself shall see the act;
  For, as thou urgest justice, be assured
  Thou shalt have justice, more than thou desirest.

SHYLOCK: I take this offer then: pay the bond thrice
  And let the Christian go.

PORTIA: Soft!
  The Jew shall have all justice; soft! No haste.
  He shall have nothing but the penalty.
  Therefore prepare thee to cut off the flesh.
  Shed thou no blood; nor cut thou less, nor more,
  But just a pound of flesh.
  Why dost the Jew pause? Take thy forfeiture.

SHYLOCK: Give me my principal, and let me go.

PORTIA: He hath refused it in the open court:
He shall have merely justice, and his bond.

SHYLOCK: Shall I not have barely my principal?

PORTIA: Thou shalt have nothing but the forfeiture,
To be so taken at thy peril, Jew.

SHYLOCK: Why, then the devil give him good of it!
(*he addresses the jury*) I am a Jew. Hath not a Jew eyes?
Hath not a Jew hands, organs, dimensions, senses,
affections, passions? Fed with the same food, hurt with
the same weapons, subject to the same diseases, healed
by the same means, warmed and cooled by the same
winter and summer as a Christian is? If you prick us,
do we not bleed? If you tickle us, do we not laugh? If
you poison us, do we not die? And if you wrong us,
shall we not revenge? If we are like you in the rest, we
will resemble you in that. If a Jew wrong a Christian,
what is his humility? Revenge. If a Christian wrong a
Jew, what should his sufferance be by Christian
example? Why, revenge. The villainy you teach me I
will execute.

This re-writing of the trial scene includes some of
Shylock's most powerful speeches in his own defence from
earlier in the play. Follow the court dramatisation with a
jury discussion where the arguments on both sides are
weighed and a verdict reached. This may be a very
different one from that which Shakespeare envisaged. You
may then wish to bring this discussion on religious
intolerance and hatred up to date and to present the story
in a different setting – perhaps in Northern Ireland or
Bosnia.

AS YOU LIKE IT (1599)

How bitter a thing it is to look into happiness through another man's eyes.

Act V Scene ii

Suggested age-group: Senior
Access: Stories in modern English
Film – *The Animated Tales*

The character of Jacques is rather unusual in Shakespeare's writing. Nowhere else do we find someone who is quite divorced from the action and who appears to simply comment on what he sees. He does, however, speak one of the most famous speeches in the Elizabethan Theatre, "All the world's a stage".

Take the speech and divide it into blocks of thought like this:

1 <u>All the world's a stage</u>,//
2 And all the men and women merely players;//
3 They have their exits // and their entrances;//
4   And one man in his time plays many parts,//
5 His acts being seven ages.//<u>At first the infant</u>,//
6 Mewling and puking in the nurse's arms;//
7 <u>Then the whining school-boy</u>//, with his satchel
8 And shining morning face,// creeping like snail
9 Unwillingly to school.// <u>And then the lover</u>,//
10 Sighing like furnace,// with a woeful ballad
11 Made to his mistress' eyebrow.// <u>Then a soldier</u>,//
12 Full of strange oaths,// and bearded like the pard,//
13 Jealous in honour,// sudden and quick in quarrel,//
14 Seeking the bubble reputation
15 Even in the cannon's mouth.// <u>And then the justice</u>,//
16 In fair round belly// with good capon lin'd,//
17 With eyes severe,// and beard of formal cut,//

18 Full of wise saws and modern instances;//
19 And so he plays his part.// <u>The sixth age shifts</u>
20 <u>Into the lean and slipper'd pantaloon,//</u>
21 With spectacles on nose// and pouch on side,//
22 His youthful hose, well sav'd,// a world too wide
23 For his shrunk shank;// and his big manly voice,//
24 Turning again toward childish treble,// pipes
25 And whistles in his sound.// <u>Last scene of all,//</u>
26 That ends this strange eventful history,//
27 Is second childishness// and mere oblivion;//
28 Sans teeth,// sans eyes,// sans taste,// sans everything.//

Begin by working with the words only. Divide the speech chorally, giving different groups of voices and solo speakers lines and see what effects you can achieve. I have underlined those phrases which are markers in the speech. These need to be used dramatically – perhaps you could try unison speaking and also solo voices. Once the students are familiar with the text begin to experiment with movement. Think about the setting – the forest of Arden. Who are the speakers going to represent? They could be characters in the play, forest-dwellers – or even trees! There are many different ways to make this speech into a dramatic performance. You could move the students only when they speak, working with levels and patterns to produce quite an abstract result. Or, more conversationally, you might decide to convey each individual age with a short mimed scene to complement the words. Consider the use of pace to show differences in age and type: perhaps the schoolboy moves slowly and reluctantly whereas the soldier is brisk. There are obvious opportunities for light and shade in vocal tone. Consider how you should convey the sounds in line 6 and lines 24 and 25. Be aware of the diminution of sound which is needed for the final line.

These are a few ideas to help you start but remember that you can adapt this format for use with any number of students. Try dividing up other famous soliloquies in this way. It is a very useful *aide memoire* for students who are required to learn speeches for examination purposes and is certainly more enjoyable than endlessly repeating the words parrot-fashion. It will also help them to feel the underlying rhythm in the blank verse. You may wish to use background music to create the mood you require.

THE TEMPEST (1611)

The isle is full of noises,
Sounds, and sweet airs, that give delight, and hurt not.

Act III Scene ii

Suggested age-group: Junior/Lower Senior
Access: Stories in modern English
    Films - *The Animated Tales*
    Prospero's Books Directed by Peter Greenaway
    1991 (suitable for seniors)
    The Tempest Directed by Derek Jarman 1980
    (suitable for seniors, some nudity)
Music: *Magic Fire* music from *The Valkyries (Die*
    Walküre) by Wagner
    Other music related to the sea – ie. *Fingal's Cave* by
    Mendelssohn
Props: Piece of blue cloth approximately two
    metres wide and four to five metres long. A
    staff for Prospero, if you wish.

I have adapted part of Act I scene ii and added Ariel's song from Act V scene i for this duologue. To set the scene we begin with a dance-drama to create the storm at sea. Listen to the *Magic Fire* music section of *The Valkyries*. You should hear a storm developing to a climax, followed by a gradual calming. Tape the music so that you can fade out at the relevant point and aim for between two and three minutes of music. Now divide the class into two groups. One group will become sprites under the control of Ariel and the other group will be the sailors on board ship, together with Prince Ferdinand.

The scene should begin with the sailors going about their business on board. Spread the cloth across the stage area behind the ship, with a sprite holding each end and the others lying on the floor behind it. Ariel casts his spell and the storm begins. The sprites whip up the sea, symbolised by the cloth which slowly waves and rises. The sailors should react to the increase in the waves with frantic activity on board ship. At the climax of the storm the cloth lifts above the heads of the sprites and they pass under it to enter the ship where they put all the sailors to sleep and Ariel leads Ferdinand, in a trance, onto dry land. The storm subsides and the cloth finishes back on the floor with the sprites. Prospero should watch the dance-drama, ideally from a higher level. At the end he comes down to meet Ariel centre stage and the duologue begins:

Storm music – Sea Dance

ARIEL: All hail, great master! Grave sir, hail! I come
    To answer thy best pleasure; be't to fly,
    To swim, to dive into the fire, to ride
    On the curl'd clouds.

PROSPERO: Hast thou, spirit,
    Perform'd to point the tempest that I bade thee?

ARIEL: To every article.
    I boarded the King's ship; now on the beak,
    Now in the waist, the deck, in every cabin,
    I flam'd amazement. Sometime I'd divide
    And burn in many places.

PROSPERO: Why, that's my spirit!
    But was not this nigh shore?

ARIEL: Close by, my master.

PROSPERO: But are they safe, Ariel?

ARIEL: Not a hair perished;
   On their sustaining garments not a blemish.

PROSPERO: Of the King's ship,
   The mariners, say how thou hast dispos'd,
   And all the rest of the fleet?

ARIEL: Safely in harbour is the King's ship.
   The mariners all under hatches stowed,
   Who with a charm joined to their suffered labour
   I have left asleep.

PROSPERO: Ariel, thy charge exactly is performed
   But there's more work.
   What is the time of day?

ARIEL: Past the mid season.

PROSPERO: The time twixt six and now
   Must by us both be spent most preciously.

ARIEL: SONG
   Where the bee sucks, there suck I;
   In a cowslips' bell I lie;
   There I couch when owls do cry.
   On the bat's back I do fly
   After summer merrily
   Merrily, merrily shall I live now
   Under the blossom that hangs on the bough.

To achieve the best results, work on the characterisations first. Ariel should use non-human movements. He is lively, quick-witted and very pleased with himself in this extract. Encourage the students to experiment with different voices. Prospero is powerful and a magical figure. Consider how he should move and speak. Think about the relationship between them and how that is manifested within the text. Ariel's song can be sung or chanted.

You can follow this by looking at the other supernatural moments in the play and by exploring the character of Caliban, who presents a real challenge for the actor who plays him.

HAMLET (1601-2)

O, what a rogue and peasant slave am I

Act II scene ii

Suggested age-group: mid to upper seniors
Access: Films: *Hamlet* directed by Laurence Olivier
1948;
Hamlet directed by Zefferelli, starring Mel Gibson
and Glenn Close 1990;
Hamlet directed by Kenneth Branagh 1997;
Animated Tales.
Play: *Rosencrantz and Guildenstern are Dead* by Tom
Stoppard.
Sound: Tape recorder and microphone
Props: Full-face white masks for the ghosts.

Begin by recording the words of the ghost of Hamlet's
father as below. If you can, use an echo machine or effect to
give the voice a supernatural quality. The tape will then be
used to speak to a student performing Hamlet's words live.
You can divide your class into pairs. One will play Hamlet
and the other will mime the part of the ghost, while wearing
a full-face mask. This is quite a difficult exercise and will
require considerable exploration of the amount of gesture
and bodily movement (particularly of the head) which is
required to show strong emotion. The students playing the
ghost need to rehearse their lines extensively so that they
are very familiar with them before using the tapes. They
need to be able to anticipate each new thought so that the
feelings can be fully shown. The scene is adapted from Act
I scene v.

Open with sound effects of wind on castle ramparts. (You
could let the students create these with their voices or use a
commercial recording).

HAMLET: Whither wilt thou lead me? Speak, I'll go no
further.

Tape of GHOST: Mark me.

HAMLET: I will.

GHOST: My hour is almost come,
When I to sulphurous and tormenting flames
Must render up myself.

HAMLET: Alas! Poor ghost.

GHOST: Pity me not, but lend thy serious hearing
To what I shall unfold.

HAMLET: Speak; I am bound to hear.

GHOST: So art thou to revenge, when thou shalt hear.

HAMLET: What?

GHOST: I am thy father's spirit;
Doom'd for a certain term to walk the night,
And for the day confined to fast in fires,
Till the foul crimes done in my days of nature
Are burnt and purg'd away. List, list, O list!
If thou didst ever thy dear father love -

HAMLET: O God!

GHOST: Revenge his foul and most unnatural murder.

HAMLET: Murder!

GHOST: Murder most foul, as in the best it is;
But this most foul, strange, and unnatural.

HAMLET: Haste me to know't, that I, with wings as swift
As meditation or the thoughts of love,
May sweep to my revenge.

GHOST: Now, Hamlet, hear:
'Tis given out that, sleeping in mine orchard,
A serpent stung me; so the whole ear of Denmark
Is by a forged process of my death
Rankly abused; but know, thou noble youth,

The serpent that did sting thy father's life
Now wears his crown.

HAMLET: My uncle!

GHOST: Ay, that incestuous, that adulterate beast,
With witchcraft of his wit, with traitorous gifts,
Oh wicked wit and gifts, that have the power
So to seduce! won to his shameful lust
The will of my most seeming-virtuous queen.
But, soft! Methinks I scent the morning air;
Brief let me be. Sleeping within mine orchard,
My custom always in the afternoon,
Upon my secure hour thy uncle stole,
With juice of cursed hebona in a vial,
And in the porches of mine ears did pour
The leperous distilment; whose effect
Holds such an enmity with blood of man
That swift as quicksilver it courses through
The natural gates and alleys of the body,
And with a sudden vigour it doth posset
And curd, like eager droppings into milk,
The thin and wholesome blood: so did it mine;
Thus was I, sleeping, by a brother's hand
Of life, of crown, of queen, at once dispatch'd.
If thou hast nature in thee, bear it not;
Let not the royal bed of Denmark be
A couch for luxury and damned incest.
                    Fare thee well at once!
The glow-worm shows the matin to be near,
And 'gins to pale his ineffectual fire;
Adieu, adieu! Hamlet, remember me.

The GHOST exits

HAMLET: Remember thee!
Ay, thou poor ghost, while memory holds a seat
In this distracted globe. Remember thee!
Yea, from the table of my memory
I'll wipe away all trivial fond records,
All saws of books, all forms, all pressures past,

That youth and observation copied there;
And thy commandment all alone shall live
Within the book and volume of my brain.
So, uncle, there you are. Now to my word;
It is "Adieu, adieu! Remember me."
I have sworn't.

Follow this with further study of the players' scene in Act III scene ii. The mime should be performed in the "grand manner" and you might like to incorporate a study of traditional mime gestures as used in Commedia dell' Arte.

MACBETH (1606)

Let not light see my black and deep desires

Suggested age-group: Senior
Access: Stories in modern English
    Film: *Macbeth* Directed by Roman Polanski 1971
    starring Jon Finch and Francesca Annis (some
    nudity);
    Macbeth directed by Trevor Nunn (RSC) with Ian
    McKellen and Judi Dench;
    Macbeth directed by Orson Welles 1942
    Animated Tales.
Music: Electronic: Jean-Michel Jarre; sound effects
    of supernatural noises and weather (*Out of this
    World* - BBC Radiophonic Workshop); percussive
    instruments.
Props: Cauldrons.

Begin by asking students to find short phrases which illustrate the dark, evil elements of the play, such as:

"blasted heath"
"infected minds"
"untimely ripp'd"
"in blood stepp'd in"

> "thick night"
> "black and deep desires"
> "blood will have blood"
> "through the fog"
> "direst cruelty"
> "dunnest smoke of hell"
> "murder sleep"

There should be enough for everyone in the class to have at least one. The students should lie on the floor with their eyes closed. Nominate a student to begin slowly chanting their line in a whisper. Others can then join in when they feel ready until you build up a sinister undertone of menace. Try continuing the chant as the class slowly gets up and moves. As students meet each other they should link their phrases and see what emotions this conveys. When you feel you have achieved an appropriate atmosphere, quieten the chant down to nothing. Now we are ready to move on to the study of the witches in groups of three. The scene should be backed by music or sound effects to create a feeling of the supernatural. Students may compose a percussive background if instruments are available.

I have amalgamated text from Act I scene i, Act I scene iii and Act IV scene i for this exercise. The character divisions have been omitted so that you can divide the speeches whichever way you wish. Aim to avoid the traditional image of three old crones circling a cauldron, chanting in unison. Perhaps your witches could be young and sensual - or one of them is prophetic and reacts strangely. They could be filthy camp followers looking for coins on the dead bodies or glamorous members of the local occult group. Think about the movement. How will you handle the objects put into the cauldron, or are they conjured up from thin air? You can use the music to invoke dance with the words incorporated between sequences or simply let it form an atmospheric backing.

> Thrice the brindled cat hath mew'd.
> Thrice and once the hedge-pig whin'd.

Harpier cries: 'tis time, 'tis time.
Fair is foul and foul is fair:
Hover through the fog and filthy air.
Round about the cauldron go,
In the poison'd entrails throw,
Toad that under cold stone
Days and nights has thirty-one
Sweltered venom sleeping got
Boil thou first in the charmed pot.

Double, double toil and trouble,
Fire burn and cauldron bubble.

Fillet of a fenny snake,
In the cauldron boil and bake.
Eye of newt, and toe of frog,
Wool of bat, and tongue of dog,
Adder's fork and blind worm's sting,
Lizard's leg, and howlet's wing –
For a charm of powerful trouble,
Like a hell-broth boil and bubble.

The weird sisters, hand in hand,
Posters of the sea and land,
Thus do go about, about:
Thrice to thine, and thrice to mine,
And thrice again, to make up nine.

Double, double toil and trouble,
Fire burn and cauldron bubble.
Scale of dragon, tooth of wolf,
Witch's Mummy, maw and gulf
Of the ravined salt-sea shark,
Root of hemlock digged in the dark,
Liver of blaspheming Jew,
Gall of goat, and slips of yew
Silvered in the moon's eclipse,
Nose of Turk, and Tartar's lips.
Fair is foul and foul is fair:
Hover through the fog and filthy air.

Finger of birth-strangled babe
Ditch-delivered by a drab –
Make the gruel thick and slab.
Add thereto a tigers chaudron
For the ingredients of our cauldron.

Double, double toil and trouble,
Fire burn and cauldron bubble.

Cool it with a baboon's blood
Then the charm is firm and good.
And now about the cauldron sing,
Like elves and fairies in a ring,
Enchanting all that you put in.
The weird sisters, hand in hand,
Posters of the sea and land,
Thus do go about, about:
Thrice to thine, and thrice to mine,
And thrice again, to make up nine.
Peace! The charm's wound up.

This scene has an interesting construction, being mainly made up of trochaic tetrameter but there is a little iambic pentameter too - can you find it?

You can move on to study other supernatural elements in the play, such as the prophecies in Act IV scene i and the appearance of Banquo's ghost in Act III scene iv.

THE TAMING OF THE SHREW (1593-94)

Fie, fie, unknit that threatening unkind brow.

Act V Scene ii

Suggested age-group: Senior
Access: Stories in modern English.
  Film: *The Animated Tales*;
  Taming of the Shrew directed by Zefferelli 1966 with
  Elizabeth Taylor and Richard Burton;
  Kiss Me Kate musical 1948 by Cole Porter.

This early play gives scope for playing broad comedy and even farce. I have taken the section of the play involving Petruchio's wooing of Katherina and their wedding, amalgamating the original text together with parts of the *Kiss Me Kate* libretto. We are not actually shown the wedding in the play but Gremio gives us a very amusing description of it in Act III scene ii. Why not write a script based on this in modern English? Use the basic scenario included in the following script. The characters should be larger than life - particularly that of Petruchio, who has tremendous confidence and panache. Katherina should show a great deal of spirit and fight in the early scene but bewilderment and fright at the wedding. Above all, have lots of fun with it!

Although the original text is in verse, I have sometimes adapted it into prose.

BAPTISTA (KATHERINA's father) and PETRUCHIO meet

PETRUCHIO: Greetings, good sir. I hear you have a daughter call'd Katherine, fair and virtuous.

BAPTISTA: I have a daughter, sir, called Katherine.

PETRUCHIO: I am a gentleman from Verona, sir, that hearing of her beauty and her wit, her affability and bashful modesty; her wondrous qualities and mild behaviour –

KATHERINA screams off

uh – mild behaviour, am bold to make myself a forward guest within your house to make mine eye the witness of that report. Signor Baptista, my business asketh haste, and every day, I cannot come to woo.

BAPTISTA: I am afraid my daughter Katherine is not for your turn, the more my grief.

PETRUCHIO: I see you do not mean to part with her. Or else you do not like my company.

BAPTISTA: Mistake me not; I speak but as I find. What may I call your name?

PETRUCHIO: Petruchio is my name; Antonio's son; a man well known throughout all Italy.

BAPTISTA: I know him well: you are welcome for his sake.

PETRUCHIO: Well, then - what dowry shall I have with her to wife?

BAPTISTA: After my death the one half of my lands.

PETRUCHIO: The fertile part?

BAPTISTA: So be it.

PETRUCHIO: And in possession?

BAPTISTA: Twenty thousand crowns.

PETRUCHIO: And, for that dowry I'll assure her of her widowhood, be it that she survives me. Let specialities be therefore drawn between us, that covenants may be kept on either hand. Go, get thee to a notary.

BAPTISTA: Signor Petruchio, will you go with me, or shall I send my daughter Kate to you?

PETRUCHIO: I pray you do, I will attend her here.

Exit Baptista

And woo her with some spirit when she comes.
Say that she rail; why then I'll tell her plain
She sings as sweetly as a nightingale.
Say that she frown; I'll say she looks as clear
As morning roses newly wash'd with dew.
Say she be mute, and will not speak a word;
Then I'll commend her volubility,
And say she uttereth piercing eloquence.
If she do bid me pack, I'll give her thanks,
As though she bid me stay by her a week;
If she deny to wed, I'll crave the day
When I shall ask the banns, and when be married.
But here she comes; and now Petruchio, speak.

Enter Katherina

Good morrow, Kate, for that's your name, I hear.

KATHERINA: Well have you heard, but something hard
of hearing. They call me Katherine that do talk of me.

PETRUCHIO: You lie, in faith; for you are called plain
Kate. And bonny Kate, and sometimes Kate the curst.
But Kate, the prettiest Kate in Christendom; and
therefore Kate, take this of me, Kate of my consolation;
Hearing thy mildness praised in every town,
Thy virtues spoke of, and thy beauty sounded,
Yet not so deeply as to thee belongs,
Myself am moved to woo thee for my wife.

KATHERINA: Moved! In good time: let him that moved
you hither
Remove you hence. I knew you at the first,
You were a moveable.

PETRUCHIO: Why, what's a moveable?

KATHERINA: A joint stool.

PETRUCHIO: Thou hast hit it. Come and sit on me.

KATHERINA: Asses are made to bear, and so are you.

PETRUCHIO: Women are made to bear, and so are you.

KATHERINA: No such jade as you, if me you mean.

She bites his hand

PETRUCHIO: Come, come, you wasp; I' faith you are
too angry.

KATHERINA: If I be waspish, best beware my sting.

She slaps him

PETRUCHIO: My remedy is then to pluck it out.

KATHERINA: Aye, if the fool could find it where it lies.

PETRUCHIO: Who knows not where a wasp does hide
his sting?
In his tail.

She slaps him again and he grabs her wrist

PETRUCHIO: I swear I'll cuff you if you strike again.

KATHERINA: If you strike me you are no gentleman.
What is your crest? A coxcomb?

PETRUCHIO: A combless cock, so Kate will be my hen.
Come give me thy hands.

KATHERINA(*struggling*): Let me go!

PETRUCHIO: Setting all this chat aside,
Thus in plain terms; your father hath consented
That you shall be my wife;
And, will you, nill you, I will marry you.
Now, Kate, I am a husband for your turn.
For by this light, whereby I see thy beauty,
Thy beauty that doth make me like thee well,
Thou must be married to no man but me.
For I am he, am born to tame you Kate;
And turn you from a wild Kate to a Kate
Conformable as other household Kates.
Here comes your father: never make denial;
I must and will have Katherine to my wife.

Baptista enters

BAPTISTA: Now, Signor Petruchio, how speed you with
my daughter?

PETRUCHIO: How but well, sir? How but well?
It were impossible I should speed amiss.

BAPTISTA: Why, how now, daughter Katherine! In your
dumps?

KATHERINE: Call you me daughter? Now, I promise you
You have show'd a tender fatherly regard,
To wish me wed to one half lunatic.

PETRUCHIO: We have 'greed so well together
That upon Sunday is the wedding-day.

KATHERINA: I'll see thee hang'd on Sunday first.

BAPTISTA: I know not what to say; give me your hands:
  God send you joy, Petruchio! 'tis a match.

PETRUCHIO: I will to Venice; Sunday comes apace:
  We will have rings, and things, and fine array;
  And kiss me, Kate, we will be married on Sunday.

  He kisses her forcefully. She slaps him and exits angrily.
  End of scene.

The Wedding Day

A crowd gathers chatting excitedly. Baptista and
Katherine enter in wedding array. There is no sign of
the bridegroom. Katherine storms off to the church.
Members of the church call out:

1　Why, Petruchio is coming in a new hat and an old
    jerkin

2　A pair of old breeches thrice turned

3　A pair of boots that have been candle-cases, one
    buckled, another laced.

4　An old rusty sword ta'en out of the town-armoury
    with a broken hilt, with two broken points.

5　His horse hipped with an old mothy saddle.

BAPTISTA: I am glad he is come, howsoe'er he comes.

PETRUCHIO: Where is Kate? Where is my lovely bride?
  How does my father? Gentles, methinks you frown:
  And wherefore gaze this goodly company,
  As if they saw some wondrous monument,
  Some comet, or unusual prodigy?

BAPTISTA: Why, sir, you know this is your wedding day.

PETRUCHIO: Ay but where is Kate? I stay too long
      from her:
  The morning wears, it is time we were at church.

BAPTISTA: But thus, I trust you will not marry her

PETRUCHIO: Good sooth, even thus; therefore ha' done
with words:
To me she's married, not unto my clothes.

He leads the crowd into church

The Service

Write your script based on this scenario.

- The priest begins the service

- At "Will you, Petruchio, take Katherina" etc Petruchio
cries, "Ay, by gog-wounds" and swears loudly

- The priest drops the prayer book in amazement

- He bends to pick it up and Petruchio slaps him hard
so that he falls over

- Petruchio says "Now take them up, if any list"

- The priest gets up with Petruchio swearing at him and
Katherina shaking with fright

- The rest of the ceremony is rushed through

- Petruchio calls for wine and toasts, "A health". He
drinks most of it and throws the dregs at a sexton
standing nearby

- He grabs Katherina and gives her a resounding kiss

Then conclude the scene as follows:

Petruchio enters leading Katherina and the guests

PETRUCHIO: Come, my bonny Kate – I said come! –
Oh Kate, content thee, I prithee be not angry.

KATHERINA: I will be angry. What has thou to do? (*she
signs to the guests*) Forward to the bridal dinner. I see a
woman may be made a fool of if she has not spirit to
resist.

PETRUCHIO: Obey the bride, you that attend on her.
Go to the feast, revel and domineer.
Carouse full measure to her maidenhead.

Be mad, be merry or go hang yourselves!
But for my bonny Kate, she must with me!
Nay, look not big, nor stamp, nor stare, nor fret.
I will be master of what is mine own.
She is my goods, my chattels; my horse, my ox, my
ass, my anything; touch her whoever dares! I'll bring
mine action on the proudest he that dares to stop my
way in Padua.

He pulls a protesting Katherina off

ROMEO AND JULIET (1595-6)

Never was a story of more woe

Act V Scene iii

Suggested age-group: Top junior/senior
Access: Stories in modern English.
   Film: *Romeo and Juliet* directed by Zefferelli in 1968
   with Leonard Whiting and Olivia Hussey;
   West Side Story 1957;
   The Animated Tales.
Music: Rock instrumental. Look at Jean-Michel Jarre,
   Mike Oldfield, Vangelis. *Romeo and Juliet* by Alec
   Costandinos and orchestra 1978. WEA Records Ltd.
Props: Fancy-dress masks, imitation daggers, two small
   bottles.

Devise a dance-drama based on the story of *Romeo and Juliet*
with the emphasis on the division of the two families.
   The whole class can work together here. First divide them
into two - the Montagues and the Capulets. You will need the
following individual characters: Romeo, Juliet, Nurse, Friar
Lawrence, Mercutio and Tybalt.
   Begin with the two factions facing each other from opposite
sides of the room. The following sequence of events works
well. Use the beats in the music to drive the action along. This
is a modern version of the story so encourage up-to-date

reactions to situations. The fight between Mercutio, Tybalt and Romeo is conducted with knives rather than swords and should be choreographed carefully to fit the music, in slow-motion at the moment Romeo kills Tybalt, so that the reactions on the faces can be clearly seen.

Dance-Drama Scenario

- Opposite each other, the two families advance until they are face to face then turn and spread out around the room

- Masks are put on and a dance commences with everyone mixing freely

- The group parts to reveal Romeo and Juliet on opposite sides of the room

- They stop and look at each other then move slowly to the centre as the others continue to dance

- Two members from each family pull them away from each other

- The group disperses to the sides leaving the Nurse and Juliet on one side, Friar Lawrence and Romeo on the other

- The Friar comes to the centre and the Nurse takes Romeo by one hand and Juliet by the other and brings them to be married. They exchange rings and embrace

- The group move in a circle round them tightly until they are absorbed

- When the group spreads out again, Mercutio and Tybalt are left in the centre fighting with knives

- As Tybalt strikes Mercutio, Romeo enters, catches his friend and lunges at Tybalt in anger with his knife – Tybalt falls and Romeo backs off in horror

- The crowd circles back in until Mercutio and Tybalt join them then spread to reveal Juliet sitting on the floor holding a small bottle

- Juliet struggles with her feelings until she gains enough strength to swallow the contents of the vial

- Two members of her family straighten her out with hands placed on her chest as if in a tomb

- Romeo enters quickly to find Juliet as if dead. He embraces her and takes out a bottle of poison which he drinks and falls by her side

- Juliet slowly awakes, sees Romeo and with great sadness takes his dagger from his belt and stabs herself

- The two families move in from opposite sides as they did at the start. This time they mix and pick up the two bodies until they lift them above their heads (carefully!)

- The funeral bearers move forward together and then off

Encourage the students to use strong facial expression and gesture to bring the action to life. You can choreograph the story exactly, using changes in the music. The students can choose the music to be used, first by listening to a variety of selections and finding the one which best reflects the story. This story is about hatred destroying love. Relate this to other modern instances of intolerance – black versus white; Catholic versus Protestant.

MUCH ADO ABOUT NOTHING (1598-9)

She speaks poniards, and every word stabs.

Act II scene i

Suggested age-group: Top junior/senior
Access: Stories in modern English
Film: *Much Ado About Nothing* directed by Kenneth Branagh 1993.
Props: Pike-staffs and lanterns.

"The Watch" represent the Elizabethan equivalent of the "Home Guard" in Britain during the Second World War. It is made up of the old, infirm and educationally challenged! This of course, means that they are guaranteed to raise a smile and the following scene gives lots of opportunities for the budding "Captain Mainwaring" or "Corporal Jones".

Dogberry is the Chief Constable – but unfortunately he doesn't quite have the command of language which his post requires. Notice the mistakes he makes: for example, he says "desartless" (undeserving) when he means deserving, "senseless" when he means the opposite, "comprehend" instead of apprehend and "tolerable" instead of intolerable!

Verges is not much better; he is rather ancient and frail and also mixes up words – saying "salvation" when he means damnation. The two members of the Watch can be as eccentric as you wish. I would recommend that you try the scene in dialect – either your local one or any other the students wish to try. It works very well in Yorkshire or Lancashire not to mention Norfolk and Somerset – or why not try "Brummy" or Welsh? If you are working abroad, you can relate the scene to your own locality. One of the funniest interpretations I have seen was given to me by a group of teachers at a workshop in Singapore entirely in "Singlish" – a delightful mixture of the local slang and basic English. So, divide your class into groups of four and enjoy creating!

This project is based on Act III scene iii.

Enter Dogberry and Verges, with the watch

DOGBERRY: Are you good men and true?

VERGES: Yea, or else it were pity but they should suffer salvation, body and soul.

DOGBERRY: Nay, that were a punishment too good for them, if they should have any allegiance in them, being chosen for the Prince's watch.

VERGES: Well, give them their charge, neighbour Dogberry.

DOGBERRY: First, who think you the most desartless man to become constable?

FIRST WATCH: Hugh Oatcake, sir, or George Seacoal; for they can write and read.

DOGBERRY: Come hither, neighbour Seacoal, God hath bless'd you with a good name. To be a well-favoured man is the gift of fortune; but to write and read comes by nature.

SECOND WATCH: Both which, Master Constable –

DOGBERRY: You have; I knew it would be your answer. Well for your favour, sir, why, give God thanks. You are thought here to be the most senseless and fit man for the constable of the Watch; therefore bear you the lantern. This is your charge; you shall comprehend all vagrom men; you are to bid any man stand, in the Prince's name.

FIRST WATCH: How, if 'a will not stand?

DOGBERRY: Why, then, take no note of him, but let him go; and presently call the rest of the Watch together, and thank God you are rid of a knave.

VERGES: If he will not stand when he is bidden, he is none of the Prince's subjects.

DOGBERRY: True, and they are to meddle with none but the Prince's subjects. You shall also make no noise in the streets; for the Watch to babble and to talk is most tolerable and not to be endured.

SECOND WATCH: We will rather sleep than talk; we know what belongs to a Watch.

DOGBERRY: Why, you speak like an ancient and most quiet watchman, for I cannot see how sleeping should offend; only, have a care that your bills be not stol'n. Well, you are to call at all ale-houses, and bid those that are drunk get them to bed.

FIRST WATCH: How if they will not?

DOGBERRY: Why, then, let them alone till they are sober; if they make you not then the better answer, you may say they are not the men you took them for.

SECOND WATCH: Well, sir.

DOGBERRY: If you meet a thief, you may suspect him, by virtue of your office, to be no true man; and, for such kind of men, the less you meddle or make with them, why, the more is for your honesty.

FIRST WATCH: If we know him to be a thief, shall we not lay hands on him?

DOGBERRY: Truly, by your office, you may, but I think the most peaceable way for you, if you do take a thief, is to let him show himself what he is, and steal out of your company.

VERGES: You have always been called a merciful man, partner.

DOGBERRY: Truly, I would not hang a dog by my will, much more a man who hath any honesty in him.

VERGES: If you hear a child cry in the night, you must call to the nurse and bid her still it.

SECOND WATCH: How if the nurse be asleep and will not hear us?

DOGBERRY: Why, then, depart in peace, and let the child wake her with crying; for the ewe that will not hear her lamb when it baes will never answer a calf when he bleats.

VERGES: 'Tis very true.

DOGBERRY: This is the end of the charge; you, constable, are to present the Prince's own person; if you meet the Prince in the night, you may stay him.

VERGE: Nay, b'yr lady, that I think 'a cannot.

DOGBERRY: Marry, not without the Prince be willing; for indeed, the Watch ought to offend no man, and it is an offence to stay a man against his will.

VERGES: By'r lady, I think it be so.

DOGBERRY: Well, masters, good night; an there be any matter of weight chances, call up me; good night. Come, neighbour.

SECOND WATCH: Well, masters, we hear our charge; let us go sit here upon the church bench till two, and then all to bed.

DOGBERRY: One word more, honest neighbours,; I pray you watch about Signior Leonato's door; for the wedding being there to-morrow, there is a great coil to-night. Adieu; be vigilant, I beseech you.

Exeunt Dogberry and Verges

Apart from the nine plays I have included here, I would also recommend for class exploration:

Julius Caesar – Act III scene ii

Twelfth Night – Act II Scene v

You may also dip into two recent publications which are particularly useful for stimulating class work. The first is *Brush Up Your Shakespeare* by Michael Macrone, published by Pavilion Books Ltd. This book takes us through the most quoted and misquoted words and phrases from Shakespeare and gives an explanation of their meanings in a light-hearted manner. It is extremely easy to dip into and come up with some fascinating facts.

The other publication is *The Shakespeare Revue* compiled by Christopher Luscombe and Malcolm McKee and published by Nick Hern Books. It is based on the Royal Shakespeare Company's show of 1994, which gathered together some of the finest comic material inspired by Shakespeare from writers as diverse as Noel Coward and Victoria Wood. You will find excellent material to introduce several of the plays I have suggested, including *Romeo and Juliet, Macbeth* and *Hamlet.* Laughter is a great way of breaking the ice and students will greatly enjoy some of the modern extracts contributed by names they are familiar with, like Stephen Fry and Hugh Laurie.

BOOK LIST

Shakespeare for Everyone (Series), Jennifer Mulherin, (Cherrytree Books)

The Cartoon Shakespeare (Series), (Sidgwick & Jackson Ltd.)

Exploring Shakespeare (Series), (Oxford University Press)

A Short Guide to Shakespeare's Plays, John Goodwin, (Heinemann)

The Pocket Companion to Shakespeare's Plays, J.C. Trewin, (Mitchell Beazley)

New Guidelines (Pamphlet on individual plays), David Self, (Mary Glasgow)

Teaching Shakespeare, Peter Reynolds, (Oxford University Press)

Starting Shakespeare, Eric Boagey, (Unwin Hyman Ltd.)

Spotlight on Shakespeare, Sandy Brownjohn & Gareth Gwyn-Jones, (Hodder & Stoughton)

Getting into Shakespeare, Theresa Sullivan, (Longman)

Production Packs (on individual plays), RSC Education Dept

EPILOGUE

Last scene of all

That ends this strange eventful history

As You Like It Act II scene vii

Shakespeare is unquestionably the greatest playwright in English literature (to date! – who can say what is yet to come?) and yet he is often avoided by teachers who feel he is "too difficult", "outdated" or "not relevant to the current syllabus". I feel that it should be every teacher's duty to instil in their students an understanding of Shakespeare's contribution to our literary history. He was, after all, a major influence on many of the writers who followed him.

Shakespeare's plays were written and performed for the ordinary people who frequented a lively, noisy, bustling theatre. The plots encompassed diverse subjects including royal intrigue, racism, love, ambition, triumph through adversity, complex relationships and the supernatural. Although the language of the plays may no longer be readily understood by all, the stories are as relevant today as they have ever been.

Shakespeare paints on a broad canvas and there is something for everyone in his plays if only we care to look. Encourage your students to see a play on stage if they can. If this is not possible then have a go yourself. Shakespeare was an ordinary man and I'm sure he would not have wished his plays to be "sacred cows" which must not be tampered with. We should find a way to make the plays accessible to youngsters so that they can begin a love of his work which will hopefully extend forward to the next generation and beyond.

USEFUL ADDRESSES

The Original Shakespeare Company
Schools Organiser
Saint Dionis' Vicarage
18 Parsons Green
Fulham
London SW6 4UH
0171 736 2585

Education Department
Shakespeare's Globe Theatre
New Globe Walk
Bankside
London SE1 9EB
0171 928 6406
0171 620 0202

The Royal Shakespeare Theatre
Waterside
Stratford upon Avon
Warks CV37 6BB
01789 296655 ext 2444

The Shakespeare Bookshop
39 Henley St
Stratford upon Avon
Warks CV37 6QW
01789 292176